Cheap Psychological Tricks

Cheap Psychological Tricks

What to Do When Hard Work, Honesty, and Perseverance Fail

Perry W. Buffington, Ph.D.

illustrated by Mitzi Cartee

PEACHTREE

ATLANTA

I am a brain, Watson.
The rest of me is mere appendix.

—Sherlock Holmes,
The Mazarin Stone,
from *Four Holmes Plays* by Michael and Molly Hardwick

Ϙ

Published by
PEACHTREE PUBLISHERS LTD.
494 Armour Circle NE
Atlanta, Georgia 30324

Text © 1996 by Perry W. Buffington
Illustrations ©1996 by Mitzi Cartee

Cover illustration by Mitzi Cartee
Cover and book design by Loraine Balcsik
Composition by Terri Fox

Manufactured in the United States of America

10 9 8 7 6 5 4 3 2 1
First Edition

Library of Congress Cataloging-in-Publication Data

Buffington, Perry W.
    Cheap psychological tricks / by Perry Buffington :
illustrated by Mitzi Cartee. —1st ed.
        p. cm.
        Includes bibliographical references.
        ISBN 1-56145-130-4 (pbk.)
        1. Psychology, Applied—Miscellanea. 2. Self-help
techniques— Miscellanea. I. Title.
BF636.B7443 1996   96-7394
158—dc20   CIP

Note from the Author

No doubt many people will question the title of this book. Allow me to say that the original title, as submitted to the editor, was *Creating Heuristic Educational and Psychological Thematics Reproducing Idiopathic, Cognitive, Kinesthetic Systems*. Surprisingly, the editor thought this title was too long, too complicated, and too much. As a result, the powers-that-be changed it.

Many thanks to my editor, Stephanie Thomas. Nothing "cheap" about her work! Couldn't have done it without you.

Perry W. Buffington, Ph.D.
(Dr. Buff)

Table of Contents

4. Re-Cycle Yourself

5. Just Between Me and Thee

6. Mind Over Matter

7. Person to Person

8. Love Is a Four-Letter Word

Introduction

Remember the last time you asked for a raise, got nothing, and then wondered what you did wrong? Too bad you hadn't learned the cheap psychological trick (CPT, for short) that almost always guarantees a raise—and often a higher raise than expected.

Or what about the last time you ate too much, then felt guilty because you overindulged? Once again, there's a cheap psychological trick that guarantees at least one bite of food will be left on your plate when you finish your meal.

Have trouble going to sleep at night? Or maybe your problem is getting up in the morning? Either way, there are some cheap psychological tricks that can help you!

With the variety of topics in this book, you're sure to find tricks that can improve your life. Topics like:
- how music influences what—and how much—you buy,
- avoiding speeding tickets,
- potty training little boys,
- using embarrassment to your advantage,
- and raising test scores without studying,

all organized by topic to make referencing easy. So jump right to the information you need, or read through the book trick by trick. All of the tricks are based on scientific research—citations are included with each entry. You're guaranteed to learn things about yourself and others that will shock, surprise, and delight you!

And *that's* no cheap psychological trick!

The material in this book is not a substitute for medical, psychological, legal, and/or other professional advice or services. This book is for entertainment only. Although it may be helpful, it is sold for informational purposes only. Neither the author nor the publisher will be held accountable for the use or misuse of the information contained in this book.

I

Quick Fixes

Cheap Trick No. 1

Be Happy – Watch Talk Shows

*A*re you happy? Would you like to be? It's easy to feel better for at least one hour a day. Try this cheap psychological trick to raise your happiness quotient. If you want to be happy, just watch daytime talk shows! This trick has to do with a psychological principle called "relative deprivation."

When the Oakland Athletics signed outfielder Jose Canseco, his pay was set at $4.7 million annually. When this happened, his teammate Rickey Henderson, who was being paid a paltry $3 million, refused to show up for spring training and questioned the "fairness" of his pay. Henderson's expectations were inflated by hearing about Canseco's pay, and his high expectations did not match his attainment, so he became unhappy.

Is there a way to consider yourself in relation to others

and be happy? Yes! Watch a daytime talk show and note all of the crazy, often depressing lives people are leading. As long as there is someone who is worse off than you (there always is—look around), and as long as you can compare yourself to that individual, you increase the probability of your being happy. This may sound like a sleazy way to go about making yourself feel better, but when you're down in the dumps, don't feel guilty about trying this trick. You aren't compounding others' problems by watching them spill their guts on television—they chose to expose themselves to the world.

What's the cheap psychological trick? Go ahead and rejoice when you see that your misfortunes are not as extensive as you think, and be grateful that your life seems completely stable and extremely happy in comparison to others' situations. Watching a talk show can make you reevaluate your position in life and reassess all the positives in it. When you count your blessings, you may find that your attainments often exceed your expectations. The result is happiness.

Think about it—if your life were as bad as it sometimes seems, you would probably already have been asked to appear as a talk show guest!

REFERENCES

Gruder, C. L. "Choice of Comparison Persons in Evaluating Oneself." *Social Comparison Processes.* Edited by J. M. Suls and R. L. Miller. New York: Hemisphere, 1977.

King, P. "Bowl players." *Sports Illustrated* March 18 (1991): 14–17.

Merton, R. K., and A. S. Kitt. "Contributions to the Theory of Reference Group Behavior." *Continuities in Social Research: Studies in the Scope and Method of the American Soldier.* Edited by R. K. Merton and P. F. Lazarsfeld. Glencoe, IL: Free Press, 1950.

Cheap Trick No. 2

The Sweet Smell of Home

You're a road warrior: takeoffs and landings, frequent flyer numbers, rental cars, hotel rooms, meetings, hotel food, taxis, airport limousines, more takeoffs and landings. You've been away from home so often your dog doesn't recognize you anymore. But travel you must, and you try to make the best of it.

You soon realize that even the nicest hotel room doesn't feel like home. The decor may be pleasant and the view may be beautiful, but it doesn't look like home. Sleeping in a different bed may be comfortable, but it's just not like sleeping at home.

Is there a way to minimize the stress of travel? The answer is yes, and the way to do it involves a cheap psychological trick and your sense of smell.

Smell is one of the most powerful senses, and it's also

one of the most primitive. Although the other senses send messages to a relay center in the brain and have them redirected to the parts of your brain responsible for those sensations, smell does not. Smell goes straight into your nostrils, and neural cells take it directly to the part of the brain responsible for interpreting smells. The sense of smell is also directly related to memory. It's not unusual for specific smells to trigger vivid memories.

What's the cheap psychological trick? If you regularly use a canned scent or potpourri that smells of cinnamon, lilac, or citrus, take this fragrance with you as you travel. Upon entering a musty-smelling hotel room, take out your "home fragrance" and spray a little of it into the air. You'll be reminded of home even as you sit in a hotel room hundreds of miles away.

This CPT also works in another way. You can use "your scent" to remind your loved ones of you while you're away on a trip. Do you use a particular cologne? If so, lightly spray some on your child's teddy bear or sleeping pillow. Spritz a little on your spouse's side of the bed. When your family goes to sleep, the scent will keep them dreaming of you.

If you are dating someone, you can do what lovers did in Victorian times. Spray your perfume or cologne on those romantic love letters before you drop them in the mailbox. (Of course, you may have people from the post office following you home, but hey, love is a risky business.) Spray your cologne or perfume on any valentines you give. You might also very lightly spray your cologne on one or two flowers in a bouquet that doesn't have a strong aroma. That way, the flower recipient will appreciate the flowers—and you—twice as much!

What's the premise behind these tricks? Smell is a powerful sense. It can cross time zones and unite you with home and loved ones even if you are thousands of miles apart. The sense of smell is directly related to memories. One "right" scent can invoke good memories and thousands of positive thoughts.

REFERENCES

Engen, T. "Remembering Odors and Their Names." *American Scientist* 75 (1987): 497–503.

Rathus, S. A. *Human Sexuality.* New York: Holt, Rinehart, and Winston, 1983.

Schab, F. R. "Odors and the Remembrance of Things Past." *Journal of Experimental Psychology: Learning, Memory, and Cognition* 16 (1990): 648–655.

Schab, F. R. "Odor Memory: Taking stock." *Psychological Bulletin* 109 (1991): 242–251.

Cheap Trick No. 3

Shopper Stoppers

Ever wonder why most stores play music—often Muzak—during shopping hours? Is it an honest attempt to make the customers more comfortable and the atmosphere of the store more pleasing? Well, not quite. In fact, the reason for the music is quite practical—slow music has been proven to sell more product.

If you always buy more items at the grocery store than you have on your list, chances are you are being actively influenced by the music supplied generously for your comfort by your grocer. When you listen to slow music, you walk slower, browse, and purchase more items. Store owners know that slower music can increase grocery purchases by about 38.2 percent.

What's the cheap psychological trick? Take along your own music. (And remember, never shop for food when you're hungry!) Plug a fast-paced cassette or CD (108 beats a minute or more) into your personal stereo and you'll spend less time shopping—and buy less, too.

Don't forget this trick when you shop by catalog. Turn off that slow music when you browse the pages—curb your spending by listening to up-tempo music.

REFERENCE
Bridgwater, C. A. "Slow Music Sells." *Psychology Today* January (1983): 56.

Cheap Trick No. 4

How to Avoid a Speeding Ticket

The best and safest advice about how to get out of a speeding ticket is simply DON'T SPEED. If, however, you are stopped for speeding and you'd like to avoid the punishment, or you feel the ticket is genuinely unfair, there are several cheap psychological tricks you can use to your advantage.

Patrol officers are taught to keep conversation to a minimum. For legal reasons this makes sense (the case may go to court, and the less said now, the better). Officers also are trained to keep their objectivity; if they talk to you, they are more likely to identify with you. In other words, trying to talk your way out of a ticket is probably not going to work. Crying can actually *increase* your chances of receiving a ticket; the officer is forced into an uncomfortable position and may want to remove him- or herself from the scene as soon as possible. It is also easier for officers to view you as a subordinate when you are bathed in tears.

The best thing you can do is try to reduce the officer's anxiety. *You* are feeling anxiety because you've been caught and another person now has control of you. The patrol person is experiencing anxiety because he or she knows nothing about you. The officer may even fear that your behavior is unpredictable. His or her life may be in jeopardy, and in these violent times, that is a very understandable apprehension. As you ease the police officer's anxiety, you will reduce the probability that you will be given a ticket.

Follow these steps:

- Stop immediately after seeing the blue lights. Your compliance will help reduce the officer's anxiety.
- As quickly as possible, show both hands. Put both hands on the steering wheel or even wave out the window. It is not necessary to hold your hands above your head; that makes you look like a criminal.
- Greet the officer and call him or her by name if identification is visible. This turns the officer into a fellow human being instead of an authority figure.
- If it looks as if you are going

to receive a ticket, ask the officer for a warning and state your reasons for leniency. *Make sure the reasons are plausible.* If you believe you were stopped unfairly, tell the officer courteously, but only after you've reduced his or her anxiety. Never argue; if you do, you immediately start a power struggle, and you will lose.

℘ If the officer gives you a warning instead of a ticket, immediately ask for directions—even if you know where you are. This turns the patrol person into a helper, something most officers would prefer to be rather than an enforcer. Providing you with directions helps him or her deal with "caving in" to your wish for a warning.

W **hat's the cheap psychological trick?** The rule is to do everything you can to reduce the officer's anxiety as quickly as possible. Your demeanor will probably be so refreshing and unusual to them that they will not see you as just another speed demon. When an officer has shown you special courtesy or fairness, write a letter of commendation to the state or local commissioner.

But why go through all this? Just don't speed unless it's a bona fide emergency.

REFERENCES
Festinger L. *A Theory of Cognitive Dissonance.* Evanston, IL: Row, Peterson, 1957.
"The Othello Error." *Science Digest* June (1988): 54–55.
Rubenstein, C. "Darth Vader on Patrol." *Psychology Today* July (1983): 72.

Cheap Trick No. 5

Teach Your Baby to Sleep Through Noise

Many new parents teasingly claim that the best time of day is when their baby is asleep. This is because the child's sleep time is the parents' down time, and the parents can temporarily regain the calmer lifestyle they led before the child was born. The parents finally have time to sit down, relax, and rest from tending the new baby. However, because of their desire to cherish this especially valued time, new parents unwittingly cause a big problem for themselves.

If new parents were familiar with one term—habituation—they could save themselves a lot of naptime grief. "Habituation" means growing accustomed to conditions in an environment, accepting them, and then blocking them out as unnoticed after a time.

When a newborn is asleep, new parents go out of their

way not to disturb the sleeping infant. They not only tiptoe around the house to avoid waking their child, they are so quiet that the child becomes used to sleeping in the silence of an "unreal" world. Children can sleep through just about anything, but if you rear them in an environment where silence is the norm, they will come to expect this silence in every sleep environment. If a child typically experiences perfect quiet when sleeping, he or she does not habituate to a pattern of everyday household noise. As a result, the child will learn to awaken to any sound.

What's the cheap psychological trick? After parents put the newborn in the crib for sleep time, they should not creep around silently. Parents should act against this instinct and immediately turn on a radio in the child's room instead.

The child will learn how to habituate to the music and get used to hearing noise while they are sleeping. As a result of the child's habituation to background noise, the parents can carry on a relatively comfortable pattern of everyday tasks and activities without waking their child. It should be possible to vacuum without waking the baby, and parents should even be able to talk in a normal tone of voice without disturbing the sleeping child. If a parent needs to work at home while the child is asleep, the phone should be able to ring without waking the child.

To refine this trick, provide a specific kind of music as the background noise for the child's sleep. Classical music is more akin to the brain's natural cycles, or electric beats per second, and it is also calming and soothing.

Put some noise in the background while the infant is sleeping, and the child will learn how to sleep more soundly. Best of all, you can stop tiptoeing!

REFERENCE

Harris, J. D. "Habituatory Response Decrement in the Intact Organism." *Psychological Bulletin* 40 (1943): 385–422.

Cheap Trick No. 6

☆Outsmart Daylight Savings Time

*T*wo times a year you are required to reset your clocks when most of the United States population either "springs forward" or "falls back."

The idea was first suggested by Benjamin Franklin, but it wasn't until World Wars I and II that changing clocks because of natural daylight patterns became a common practice. At that time it was important to conserve energy for the war effort. Today, daylight savings time exists more for our enjoyment of daylight hours than anything else... but nature demands a payback!

Setting a watch back is easy, but resetting (or technically speaking, "entraining") our internal clocks is a bit more problematic. As you probably know from having jetlag, it takes our bodies a while to adapt to a different time zone. The same is true when we must adjust to daylight savings time.

Americans are asked to change their clocks at 2:00 A.M. on Sunday. The next day, Monday, people resume their work routines, but their body clocks are lagging behind. On the day after the time changes (either springing forward or falling back) accidents increase by about 20 percent because all those bodies are struggling to catch up.

To give yourself an extra edge, instead of resetting your clock on Sunday morning, either spring forward or fall back one day early, at 2:00 A.M. on Saturday. (Unless you are a night owl, you will actually reset your clocks before you go to sleep Friday night.)

What's the cheap psychological trick? Springing forward two days before the new time commences gives your body ample time to adjust body rhythms to the new schedule. On Monday morning when the rest of the world feels sluggish and lethargic, you will be rested and alert.

This approach can help children adjust smoothly, too. Reset their clocks two days before the Monday of the school week so their internal clocks will be reset as well. Other children in the class may feel unusually sleepy, but your kids will be bright-eyed and bushy-tailed.

REFERENCES

Moore-Ede, Martin C., Frank M. Sulzman, and Charles A. Fuller. *The Clocks that Time Us.* Cambridge, Massachusetts: Harvard University Press, 1982.

Vollmer, R. "Spring Forward, Fall Back." *Psychology Today* September (1983): 18.

Cheap Trick No. 7

Ride a Roller Coaster Without Puking

Take a quick test and name the body's senses. Most people list seeing, smelling, tasting, hearing, and touching. But you failed the test if you listed only these basic five senses. There are two others: the *kinesthetic* and *vestibular* sensory systems.

When you are asked to close your eyes and touch your nose with your index finger, you are engaging the kinesthetic sensory system; sense receptors located in your joints, tendons, and muscles inform your head about various positions and movements of bodily parts. Individuals whose movements have been dramatically impaired as a result of accidents are well aware of the value of this sensory information. If you were to contract your bicep and couldn't use your kinesthetic senses, you would have to look at your arm or touch your muscle to know that the message "contract the bicep" successfully made it from your brain to your arm.

The other special sense, the vestibular, signals balance and offers information as your head rotates through space in relation to gravity. A gymnast flipping through the air is relying on kinesthetic and vestibular senses more than on vision. The vestibular sense organ is located in the inner ear. If you were riding in a car blindfolded, this sense would tell you when you are speeding up or slowing down. This is also the mechanism that tells you when you are falling or going up or down in an elevator, and it's also the culprit behind motion sickness.

These two special senses get a real workout when you are on an amusement park ride, particularly one that turns you in all directions. How can knowledge of your senses help reduce the chances of throwing up after an amusement park ride? Use this information to trick your brain.

Look straight ahead when you are on a roller coaster, or look in the direction of the spin if the ride travels in a circular motion. Don't shut your eyes—if you do, all of the information your brain will receive will come from the kinesthetic and vestibular senses, and those delicate mechanisms are easily discombobulated!

Seventy percent of all the information that reaches your brain comes from your vision. Using your vision to stabilize your kinesthetic and vestibular senses will minimize the chances of being sick. The simplest way to combine your sense of vision and your kinesthetic and vestibular senses is always to look in the direction in which the ride is moving.

If you have a tendency to be carsick when you sit in the back seat, sit in the middle of the seat and look straight ahead. In this position, your sense of vision will relay 70 percent of the information about your movement through space, and your special senses will only be required to provide the remaining 30 percent. Again, your chances of becoming sick will drastically decrease. Following the same logic, people prone to carsickness should avoid keeping their gazed fixed on a book or turning around to talk to backseat riders during a long trip.

What's the cheap psychological trick? On any amusement park ride, look straight ahead or in the direction of the spin. If you close your eyes or look in the opposite direction, you may find yourself losing your lunch when the ride stops.

REFERENCES

Coon, D. *Introduction to Psychology: Exploration and Application.* Los Angeles: West Publishing Company, 1983.

Panati, C. *Breakthroughs.* New York: Berkley Books, 1980.

Rathus, S. *Psychology.* New York: Holt Rinehart, and Winston, 1981.

"States of Mind: Seeing is Deceiving." *Psychology Today* March–April (1996): 24.

2

Nose
to the
Grindstone

$ $ $

Cheap Trick No. 8

Survive Public Speaking

Public speaking can terrify even the most stalwart. It's right up there with taxes and the dentist on the list of things we love to hate. Throw a heckler into the crowd, and the situation worsens; mean-spirited questions can reduce even the most prepared speaker to tears. Performers and professional lecturers deal with interrupters by outsmarting them, but that's not so easy for the rest of us to manage. Fortunately, there is an easier way to pull through this situation, and it works 99.99 percent of the time. All it takes is a CPT to gain the upper hand.

Say you are at a business meeting. You're doing a wonderful job presenting your side of the "Hoppity-Floppity Bunny Rabbit" toy sale projections. Then, out of the blue, someone starts questioning every step of the campaign, throwing out inappropriate or disparaging remarks. If you put down the heckler in a sarcastic tone, you'll look like the bad guy and the heckler will come away from the conflict unscathed.

So what should you do to get out of this mess? Nothing. That's right—do nothing. If someone verbally jumps on you, resist the urge to jump back. Instead, take a deep breath and say nothing. Let someone in the audience enter the fray on your behalf and take on the heckler for you.

Why is this a good strategy? Remember that the majority of people hate public speaking. The others in the room are incredibly grateful that they aren't in your shoes. They are rooting for you because they, too, have the same fear of public speaking lurking in the deep dark recesses of their conscious and unconscious brain. When someone verbally attacks you or your argument, they vicariously feel your pain. As the pain builds inside of the audience, chances increase that some brave soul will enter the discussion to defend your point or to respond to the heckler's remarks.

This trick also works when you don't know the answer to a question. Before you admit, "I don't know," allow time for someone in the room to come to your rescue. When that person has answered the question, you can say, "I agree with you, and furthermore..." When you add your own point, your not-knowing-the-answer silence will look like a thoughtful pause.

What's the cheap psychological trick? When it looks like your public-speaking career is faltering and others are identifying with your emotional discomfort, wait for some kind soul to come to your rescue. Do nothing, and you'll survive to speak in public again!

REFERENCES

Eisenberg, N., and R. Lennon. "Sex Differences in Empathy and Related Capacities." *Psychological Bulletin* 94 (1983): 100–131.

Hall, J. A. "On Explaining Gender Differences: The Case of Nonverbal Communication." *Review of Personality and Social Psychology* 7 (1987): 177–200.

"Public Speaking Addressing Fears." *Psychology Today* May–June (1996): 11.

"These Are a Few of Our Scariest Things." *Psychology Today* March (1989): 14.

Cheap Trick No. 9

Get the Raise You Deserve

Number one (and *no* trick, psychological or not, will get you a raise without this step): You have to *ask* for what you want! If you want a raise, you must ask for it. It isn't easy, but once you make the decision to ask the big question, these techniques can increase your chances of getting a raise.

Before you confront your employer, stand in front of the mirror and rehearse, "I *deserve* a raise." Never say, "May I have a raise?," "Could I have a raise?," or "Is it time for my raise?" Always say, "I *deserve* a raise." Make a list of reasons you deserve a raise. Write down exactly what you have done to deserve the raise. Stick to observable achievements that cannot be disputed. If a dollar value in savings to the company has resulted from your work, make sure you have documentation confirming this at your fingertips.

Now—concerning the a-
mount of the raise. Always ask
for *more* than you think you deserve. The key word here is
"more." Rehearse this higher
amount while standing in
front of a mirror so you won't
hesitate or stutter when you
ask your boss for the raise.

The average worker goes in
and asks for a modest raise, un-
aware that this simple, low-raise
request may have negative side effects.
When a worker asks for a very small
raise, the employer has a tendency to
devalue the employee. It's just a screwy quirk of human nature. (People who frequently have garage sales know that pro-
spective buyers are just as likely to be turned off by an object
priced too low as by an overpriced one.)

However, when you ask for a reasonably higher raise, then
you trigger a new thought process in your employer's head.
The new thought that you are worth more makes the employer
more open to an honest evaluation of your value to the company. Even if you don't get the higher increase in raise you
requested, you'll probably find that work conditions improve.
Why? The boss will treat you differently because he or she
now sees you in a new and brighter light. If you want to be
treated like dirt, then never ask for anything or just ask for a
tiny raise—you'll probably get the worst assignments, the

lousiest office, the most distant parking space, and the longest hours. After all, if you don't see yourself as valuable—you have suggested this by the low amount of money you have asked for—why should your boss?

An impression of your ability and your worth, as well as an idea of what size raise (if any) you deserve, already exists in your employer's mind. If you give well-documented reasons why you are valuable to the company, this new information will conflict with the preconceived notions in your boss's head. (This is called "cognitive dissonance.") Your boss must then reconcile these two conflicting perceptions. Until you present this conflict, this "dissonance," your boss will keep the old idea of your worth. The conflicting information, however, will force the employer to reevaluate you and act on the new revised image of you as an employee.

What's the cheap psychological trick? Upon entry to an organization, ask for a higher salary than you think you need or deserve. At raise time, ask for a higher raise than you think you need or deserve. Even though you may be willing to accept less cash, asking for a higher amount may improve your employer's perception of you.

REFERENCES
Festinger L. *A Theory of Cognitive Dissonance.* Evanston, IL: Row, Peterson, 1957.
Half, Robert. *Finding, Hiring, and Keeping the Best Employees.* New York: John Wiley & Sons, 1993.
Half, Robert. "How to Ask for a Raise Without Getting Fired." *Bottom Line Personal* June 15 (1993): 12.
Meer, Jeff. "Bid High, But Not Too High." *Psychology Today* July (1985): 66.

Cheap Trick No. 10

Motivating Others to Do What You Want

Your employee just doesn't seem to get the hang of his job. He can never decide how to go about getting the task at hand completed. Is there a way to motivate him to do what you want done? Your committee is spinning its wheels. Is there something you can do to give it traction? Your child is demanding a chocolate bar, but you don't want to give her candy. Can you satisfy her with a more nutritious snack—without a battle of wills?

The answer to all of these questions is *yes*, and you can successfully control these situations by mastering the phenomenon of options. Let's see how a savvy boss handles a touchy situation.

There's a difficult project at hand, and you are the one in charge. There's no way you can oversee all the day-to-day elements of the project, and you need the help of your assistant.

How can you motivate your assistant to take over an important part of the project without losing control of the direction of the effort as a whole? One of the best ways to lead others is to give them choices. Approach your assistant and say, "As you know, we have this project with these problems. I think you are the one to handle this aspect of the project. Use Method A or Method B and run with it."

Who's in control here? Your assistant thinks that he or she is, but the truth is that you, the person who set up the choices, are the one in control.

Employees who are given choices feel empowered. The feeling of control will increase their commitment to the job and company, and perhaps lower absenteeism rates. Even with the additional responsibilities, stress levels are likely to decrease because of the added sense of control.

Be aware, though, that if you give your charge three choices—Method A, Method B, or Method C—his or her stress level will probably go *up*. With three options to choose from, workers are faced with a dilemma: which of the choices is good, better, and best? His or her sense of control diminishes.

If your committee has been discussing a new project for hours and can't seem to settle on a course of action, bring up two resolutions that you think would work the best and call for a vote. The committee will then have a clear choice and can feel good about getting the job done.

If your daughter is screaming for chocolate and you say, "No," she will most likely only scream louder. If you nix the chocolate and then add, "You can have a banana or some strawberries," the child must rethink her demands and re-evaluate the situation. The same technique can work when your child wants to choose which clothes to wear on an important occasion. Offer two choices and give the child the responsibility of picking which one to wear. (But be warned: children are often more attuned to manipulation than adults; this trick may not work repeatedly!)

W **hat's the cheap psychological trick?** When you give someone a choice, you take that person's mind off the original problem and offer leadership and guidance in the guise of handing over responsibility.

REFERENCES
Bennis, W. "Transformative Power and Leadership." *Leadership and Organizational Culture.* Edited by T. J. Sergiovani and J. E. Corbally. Urbana: University of Illinois Press, 1984.
Rodin, J. "A Sense of Control" [interview]. *Psychology Today* December (1984): 38–45.

Cheap Trick No. 11

Wow Others With Hidden Knowledge

Here is a CPT that underlings use to impress their superiors and that children expertly apply to surprise their parents.

Imagine a business setting in which you must make an oral presentation. There will be people in the room who you feel are adversaries rather than team members—people who will likely be looking for weaknesses in your plan.

In your written memo to the people who will attend the meeting, allude briefly to an important issue, but leave out details or explanations. Your adversaries will spend most of their time planning a destructive strategy around something they think you have obviously overlooked. When they gleefully raise the issue, you can immediately pull out an overhead, wield the pointer, and shine brighter with answers than the light on the projector! Your opposition will think twice before they try to undermine you again. You can use this CPT to control other situations as well. Feigning ignorance, then showering others with facts, can come in handy during job interviews, contract negotiations, or oral exams—anytime you want to manipulate another person's opinion.

Children know this trick and use it to their advantage. They "forget" to tell you that they know something, then spontaneously wow you with their knowledge at an unexpected moment in order to gain praise or tangible signs of your approval.

Take the following situation: you are overseeing your son's birthday party, and everything is running along smoothly. The children are all behaving, and your son is being a little gentleman. After everyone sings "Happy Birthday" and the applause dies down, your son launches into a "Happy Birthday" solo...in Russian. You are shocked and grinning with pride. You had no idea that he knew how to sing in Russian, much less that he had the inclination to perform in public.

You are the victim of a CPT; whatever the precocious soloist wants for the next hour or so, he shall have—from everyone in the room! (As you may be able to tell, this is a true story and a painful case of being manipulated with your own trick.)

What's the cheap psychological trick? Omit vital information, allow your audience to think that you don't know certain facts, or both. If they are critics, they will waste no time trying to expose your "ignorance." When you answer with alacrity, you become an expert in the eyes of the onlookers, and anyone who has tried to trip you up comes across as a bully. If you can present valuable information or perform an amazing feat when others least expect it, you will greatly increase the impact of your accomplishment.

REFERENCES

Piaget, J. *The Origins of Intelligence in Children.* New York: Norton, 1963.
Piaget, J. *The Construction of Reality in the Child.* New York: Ballantine, 1971.

Cheap Trick No. 12

Pull an All-Nighter

very once in a while, it's necessary to stay up all night. Whether you're pulling an all-nighter to meet a deadline for an important corporate project or to cram for an exam, it's usually difficult to trick your body into cooperating with your need to stay awake. Researchers have found a way to help, and it's a cheap *physiological* trick. ("Consult your physician before you try any physical tricks," quoth my attorney.)

The best approach is to plan your work schedule to avoid a last-minute crisis, but if you must stay up all night, you may want to consider this method. It's a combination of naps and caffeine. (Caffeine can work wonders on the human clock. It's actually in a class of chemicals called "zeitgebers," or "time givers.")

What's the cheap psychological trick? Follow these steps to make it through to "dawn's early light":

$ Take a four-hour nap early in the evening.

$ Hit the coffee or other caffeinated drink of your choice; drink about two cups between midnight and 1:30 A.M. and another two cups between dawn and 7:30 A.M.

$ Congratulate yourself for staying up all night and meeting the deadline.

Researchers found one little catch to this method. It works for one night, but the body's natural sleep mechanism takes over the following night.

Do this when you must, but don't become dependent on sleep deprivation to get things done! Your body will eventually find a way to pay you back.

REFERENCES

Browman, C. P., K. S. Gujavarty, M. N. Mitler, and M. G. Sampson. "The Drowsy Crowd." *Psychology Today* August (1982): 35–38.

Gulevich, G., W. C. Dement, I. Johnson. "Psychiatric and EEG Observations on a Case of Prolonged (264 Hours) Wakefulness." *Archives of General Psychiatry* 15 (1966): 29–35.

"How to Stay Up All Night." *Health* October (1994): 12.

Moore-Ede, Martin C., Frank M. Sulzman, and Charles A. Fuller. *The Clocks that Time Us.* Cambridge, Massachusetts: Harvard University Press, 1982.

Cheap Trick No. 13

It's Not What You Know...

ere's a question that has always plagued information scientists: which is more important, *who* you know or *what* you know? Many people—especially parents—advise others to get a good education if they want to go far in life. Some people, however, choose the route of "brown-nosing," "apple polishing," or "toadying" up to someone whom they believe may hold the key to their success. Which really is more important, who or what you know?

The most important thing seems to be *who* you know. Statistics from information theorists show that *what* you know is important 12.5 percent of the time, but *who* you know is important 87.5 percent of the time.

So, how do you get to the "who" you want to meet? Well, that's a CPT. No matter who you want to know, information theorists propose that you are a maximum of six people away from meeting them—in most cases fewer than that. Consider this hypothetical situation: You want to meet the president of the United States. You probably know someone (an uncle, for example) who knows a petty bureaucrat in your city. The bureaucrat may be best friends with the deputy counsel for agricultural affairs, who often talks to the undersecretary of spin analysis, who is having an affair with a White House staff member, who knows the president's assistant, who can potentially help you get in to meet the president. In this case, you are a mere six people away from the president.

W **hat's the cheap psychological trick?** Now that you know you are within a chain of six people (usually fewer) connecting you to anyone you want to meet, start right away to look for those people who can "get you in." Very few people are unapproachable. You just have to find that first person on the chain and work your way up. This one simple observational statistic encouragingly suggests that the world really is a small place, and any one person can make a connection to any other.

Once you're in, you're back to the old advice: "Get an education and you will go far." If you can't prove yourself, it doesn't matter who you know (unless you're a born genius with unlimited inherited wealth). See, your mother was right all along!

REFERENCE
Guare, J. *Six Degrees of Freedom*. New York: Vintage Books, 1990.

Cheap Trick No. 14

Raise Your Test Scores – Without More Study

The very best way to raise your test scores is to study, study, study. In fact, some evidence suggests that studying one hour past the point where you *think* you know the material can raise your grade by one letter. But no matter how much you study, some exams will include information you've never seen in your life. When that happens, it's good to know a couple of cheap psychological tricks that can increase the probability of answering the question correctly.

If the instructor gives you a "stem" phrase or question and then requires you to pick one correct answer, either A, B, C, or D (a multiple-choice test), you can increase your chances of guessing the right answer even if you don't know anything about the subject matter.

W **hat's the cheap psychological trick?** If you haven't a clue which choice is the correct answer, pick the longest one. Teachers have a subconscious tendency to make the longest item the correct one. They may also reason that giving a plethora of information will minimize the probability that students will complain about misleading choices or unfair grading.

Other tricks to remember:

- § If most of the multiple-choice questions contain four choices, but occasionally a fifth choice is thrown in, 80 percent of the time the fifth choice is the correct answer.
- § If one of the choices is overly technical, that item is probably *not* the correct one.
- § When opposites appear among the answers, one of them is usually correct.
- § When two of the choices are almost identical in their wording, one of these similar choices is often the correct one.

But what if the test isn't multiple choice? The CPTs for other types of exams aren't quite as specific, but may give you the edge you need. Make sure you dress lightly, and don't eat much before the test. Some evidence suggests that you perform best when you are slightly cool (about 65 degrees) and a little hungry. These two factors are thought to increase alertness and concentration.

Another hint: Never show up for an exam early. Before a test begins, people tend to gather together and review the material to be tested. If someone asks questions you don't know, your anxiety is likely to soar, decreasing your test performance. **39**

If you arrive early, review your notes alone, and try to relax before the test begins.

Remember: The best psychological trick of all is to be prepared!

REFERENCES
"Beyond I.Q." *Psychology Today* September (1979): 25.
Brown, F. G. *Measuring Classroom Achievement.* New York: Holt, Rinehart, & Winston, 1981.
Goleman, D. "The New Competency Tests: Matching the Right People to the Right Jobs." *Psychology Today* January (1981): 35.
Rice, B. "Brave New World of Intelligence Testing." *Psychology Today* September (1979): 27–41.
Sternberg, R. J. "A Shortcut to Problem Solving." *Psychology Today* September (1979): 47.
Sternberg, R. J. "Stalking the I.Q. Quark." *Psychology Today* September (1979): 42–54.

Cheap Trick No. 15

Think Faster — And Better!

If your last name begins at the first part of the alphabet, you've probably learned how to think fast without even realizing it. Many teachers—past and present—call on students based on their ranking in the alphabet. As a result, when the teacher asks a question, the first "A" in the alphabet has to think fast, while the person whose last name begins with "Z" has quite a while to mull it over. (In some cases, the "Z" can ponder dozens of other answers before being called on!)

It's common sense—and sound psychology—that behaviors we learn in childhood come with us into adulthood. If you are required to answer quickly when you're a child, you'll come up with answers faster when you're an adult, even if just out of habit.

But what if you are one of those end-of-the-alphabet

thinkers with an "untrained brain"? Can you learn how to think fast after years of being last in line? That's where this CPT comes in.

Stand up.

Sounds too simple? Well, it *is* just that simple. Humans think faster—some say as much as 20 percent faster—when they are standing up. Why? Standing increases a person's heart rate by about ten beats per minute. The increased heart rate stimulates activity in the brain centers. Here's how this trick can work for you:

$ The next time you make a presentation, sit until it is time for you to begin speaking. Then stand and stay standing, especially through any question-and-answer session. You'll have an edge over those who have become comfortable in their chairs. (You'll also benefit from the psychological advantage of height, because the people seated must look up to you.)

$ When you make telephone cold calls, stand up and you'll be quicker, more alert, and better able to win others over to your point of view.

$ When you take an oral quiz, ask to stand as you recite your answers.

$ Choose amusement park rides that require you to stand.

The ride will thrill you more because of your heightened alertness.

What's the cheap psychological trick? Stand up when you need to think fast; as your heart rate picks up, your brain will work better!

REFERENCES

Fozard, J. L., M. Vercruyssen, S. L. Reynolds, and P. A. Hancock. "Age Differences and Changes in Reaction Time: The Baltimore Longitudinal Study of Aging." *Journals of Gerontology* 49 (1994): 179–189.

Morgan, B. S. "A Contribution to the Debate on Homogamy, Propinquity, and Segregation." *Journal of Marriage and the Family* 43 (1981): 909–921.

•••••• 3 ••••••

Physical Therapy

Cheap Trick No. 16

Telling Glances

In every waking moment, your eyes send a clear-cut and straightforward message about you to the world. Learn to read the messages in the eyes of the people around you, and you will gain new insight into their inclinations and motivations.

The science of "pupillometrics"—the measurement of change in the diameter of pupils in the eyes—has yielded some fascinating information about the connection between feelings and eye physiology.

Here's how the connection works. Your sensory organs respond to your emotions and interests. If you see something you like, your pupils dilate, or get bigger. If something offends you, your pupils tend to constrict or shrink in size. Pay attention to people's eyes; you can learn a lot about how they feel.

Playing a poker game with big stakes? Are you playing with gamblers who have mastered the true poker face? Chances are, they haven't perfected the art of "poker eyes." Watch them as their hands are dealt. If they like their hands, their pupils will "tell" on them by dilating. If they don't like their cards, their pupils will constrict and reveal their displeasure, even as they maintain their poker faces.

Feeling hungry? Your eyes will tell on you. When you are famished, your pupils will open up in the presence of food.

Afraid of rejection? Watch people you like as you talk with them. Do they gaze into your eyes? Did their pupils dilate when they met you? If so, go for it! They'll go out with you or buy your product. In fact, they'll do just about anything you ask (okay, maybe that's taking things a little far, but you get the idea).

Research also has been done on the significance of the eye movements people make when pondering a question. You've probably never noticed, but when you ask someone for an answer, they tend to break gaze with you and shift their eyes either left or right. This involuntary movement does not appear in children until they are three or four years of age, when they have learned verbal expression. (Individuals diagnosed as severely disturbed emotionally or mentally retarded tend not to shift their gaze. However, blind individuals who exhibit sound verbal skills *will* shift their gaze.)

If someone asks you a question and your gaze shifts to the right, you probably tend to be rather anxious, possibly fearful. This fear prods you to make fast decisions. You are also more external or action-oriented. If you were hungry you would probably say, "I've got to get food." If your gaze shifts to the left, you are generally more subjective and feeling-oriented and less action-oriented. If food were mentioned, you might say, "I feel hungry." (A bit of eye movement trivia: Husbands and wives tend to be opposite gazers. That is, if the wife is a right gazer, then the chances are high that the husband is a left gazer.)

What's the cheap psychological trick? Watch those eyes. When people's pupils expand, they're thinking "yes." But when pupils shrink, back off and wait for a more opportune time to approach. If you must persuade someone who is a right gazer, offer them cold, hard facts. If the person is a left-gazer, base your appeal on feelings. If you don't want others to use these tricks on you, wear sunglasses!

REFERENCES

Day, M. E. "Don't Teach Until You See the Direction of their Eye Movements." *The Journal of Special Education* 4 (1978): 233–237.

Degliantoni, L. "Illusions of Grandeur." *Psychology Today* May–June (1996): 22.

"Mental Illness: The Eyes Have It." *Science News* April 20 (1983): 124, 126.

Cheap Trick No. 17

Pee in Public (For Men Only)

Women reading this topic may think it is funny, but men know it's no laughing matter. Although women have a stall to hide them from strangers in the bathroom, men are required to saunter up to the urinal, create a quick flow, flush, and then let the next person have a go, all without a bit of privacy. The quicker the better; the faster the better; the less said the better.

Little boys—assuming they can reach the urinal—can urinate just about anywhere without any problem. By adolescence, however, many boys are so inhibited and self-conscious that they simply can't do it in public. As adults, many males freeze, mentally taunted by childhood sayings like, "Players with short bats step close to the plate," sometimes opting to "hold it" until they get home to a safe environment.

Researchers devised a rather ingenious method to determine how stress and high levels of arousal interfered with men's use of urinals. They found that arousal of any kind can interfere with a man's ability to urinate, a problem technically referred to as "delay of onset" of flow.

Here's the scene: Imagine a men's room with three urinals and one walled toilet stall.

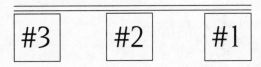

If it was set up so that man A chose to use urinal #1, two scenarios are possible. Man B could come in and use urinal #2—the urinal next to man A. He could also choose urinal #3 and leave an unused urinal in the middle. What happened in the study when a "space invader" chose the urinal right next to man A? The poor man couldn't urinate as quickly or as much! Some men couldn't urinate at all, and many faked and stood before the urinal for a short time, then zipped their flies, washed their hands, and walked out. They often came back when they thought the crowd or waiting line had gone away.

Standing before the urinal until the flow starts, no matter how long it takes, typically will not help men overcome urinal fears. In fact, the more frequently they are unable to urinate in public, the more their anxieties increase.

What's the cheap psychological trick? The first one is quite simple: whistle. This may sound simplistic, but it works. Whistling takes your mind off the task at hand and lets your body take over automatically.

Another trick that works is adopting an aggressive posture. Keep others from using the urinal next to you by intimidating them. Let them worry about the "delay of onset." The next time you belly up to the urinal, extend your member. Once it is securely pointed (you don't want to drip on your clothes), place both hands on your hips. Just imagine someone walking in to use the urinal and seeing you standing there doing your business, not holding on, just letting it all hang out, with both hands on your hips. Anyone can see that you have staked out your territory, and you've earned the extra space of the urinal next to you.

If these tricks don't work for you, avoid liquids during meetings or use the stall!

REFERENCES

Karabenick, S. A., and M. Meisels. "Effects of Performance Evaluation on Interpersonal Distance." *Journal of Personality* 40 (1972): 275–276.

Koocher, G. P. "Bathroom Behavior and Human Dignity." *Journal of Personality and Social Psychology* 35 (1977): 120–121.

Middlemist, R. D., E. S. Knowles, and C. F. Matter. "Personal Space Invasions in the Lavatory: Suggestive Evidence for Arousal." *Journal of Personality and Social Psychology* 33 (1976): 541–546.

Middlemist, R. D., E. S. Knowles, and C. F. Matter. "What to Do and What to Report: A Reply to Koocher." *Journal of Personality and Social Psychology* 35 (1977): 122–124.

Cheap Trick No. 18

Need a Pick-Me-Up? Take a Hike!

*A*re you sagging and in need of a quick pick-me-up? Thinking about eating a chocolate bar? Wait, before you run to the snack machine, consider a better way to give yourself a boost—it's nonfattening, and this CPT won't cost you a thing!

As physiologists point out, a candy bar *will* elevate your mood immediately, but about half an hour later, you will be more tired than you were when you ate it, and you'll also be more tense. To add insult to injury, for this extra tension, you paid about a buck. Why not take a ten-minute walk instead?

In a bad mood? Take a short walk and feel your gloomy outlook brighten. It doesn't matter if it's a jaunt on a treadmill in a bare-walled room or a real nature hike with a scenic view. Your reward will be renewed energy, mental as well as physical.

Had a rough day? Making the transition from one project to the next? Need to clear your head? Try a ten-minute walk.

Why is this technique so powerful? In addition to positive physiological effects—increased heart rate, deeper breathing, and stimulated muscles—a walk can provide mental benefits as well. When you are thinking about your walk, where you're walking, and how long you'll walk, you're not thinking about work or your troubles; your mind can shift gears. A simple walk clears your head while it exercises your body.

- Are you about to lose your temper? Take a hike. A simple ten-minute walk can do wonders to restore a sense of balance.
- Would you like to get to know someone better? Ask a new acquaintance to take a ten-minute walk with you. It's amazing how walking with someone can bring you closer.
- Do you have a difficult assignment you must complete? One that's psychologically or physiologically taxing? If you take periodic breaks and an occasional ten-minute walk you will accomplish your task more efficiently.

What's the cheap psychological trick? A brisk walk gives your mind and your body energy. What is often more important, however, is that when you're walking toward something, you tend to forget what you're walking away from!

REFERENCE
Thayer, R. E. "Energy Walks." *Psychology Today* October (1988): 12–13.

Cheap Trick No. 19

Spill Your Guts!

Keeping emotional pain inside is like bandaging an unwashed wound—both practices invite infection. For years, psychologists have suggested that patients write a never-to-be-sent letter to those who anger or hurt them as a way of venting their feelings. Now this form of therapy seems to have applications in the medical realm as well. Although most physicians haven't begun to prescribe letter-writing to their patients, research increasingly suggests that this sort of self-medication not only helps the mind, but also benefits the body.

The connection between stress and illness has long been accepted by both medical and psychological doctors; stress can weaken many aspects of the immune system. In one experiment, scientists set out to measure the effects of stress on the immune system by studying a group of students asked to complete three different tasks. After recording the subjects' beginning levels of immunity, the scientists divided the group into three sections. They asked the first group of students to go into separate rooms and write down any boring, innocuous information that came to their heads, like a list of the clothes hanging in their closets. The second group went into identical rooms, where each individual was instructed to write a letter about a painful personal episode he or she had never told anyone about, explaining the hurt they carried around and its lack of resolution. The third group went into rooms where they were asked to relate the same sort of negative episode in narrative form as Group Two, but instead of writing a letter, they talked about the incident into a tape recorder.

The scientists measured each group's level of immunity after the completion of the exercises to determine what, if any, effect these actions had on the subjects' immune systems. As you might expect, Group One showed no change in the performance levels of their immune systems. The students in Group Two, however, showed noticeable increases in their immune system functioning. Group Three outdid even Group Two's improvement, with immune systems that demonstrated remarkable positive affects. This study suggests that writing a letter to yourself is good for body and mind, but speaking personal pain aloud can produce tangible mental and physical benefits.

What's the cheap psychological trick? The simple action of revealing inner pain to yourself through writing or speaking can produce dramatic improvements in your immune system. The reasons behind this phenomenon are somewhat difficult to pin down. Perhaps the act of writing or speaking aloud about a traumatic event forces the brain to organize it, which in turn reduces the number of stress-provoking thoughts spinning around and around in a person's head. Even though you don't know exactly how it works, you can use this cheap trick to clear your conscience and increase the performance of your immune system in one step.

REFERENCES

Berry, D. S., and J. W. Pennebaker. "Nonverbal and Verbal Emotional Experience and Health." *Psychotherapy and Psychosomatics* 59 (1993): 11–19.

Esterling, B. A ., M. H. Antoni, M. A. Fletcher, S. Margulies, and N. Schneiderman. "Emotional Disclosure through Writing or Speaking Modulates Latent Epstein-Barr Virus Antibody Titers." *Journal of Consulting and Clinical Psychology* 62 (1994): 130–140.

Cheap Trick No. 20

The Perfect Night's Sleep

How did you sleep last night? When you put your head on your pillow, did you go straight to sleep or were you suddenly wide awake? It has been estimated that as many as 40 percent of Americans will suffer from some form of sleep disturbance at one time or another. If you have trouble sleeping—or waking up—this is the CPT for you.

Before we begin, answer these questions and solve an easy math problem:

- Do you wake up alert or groggy?
- How many hours do you sleep on an average night?
- Do you use a snooze alarm?
- Take the number of hours you sleep and divide it by 1.5.

First, let's discuss how sleep works. We sleep in ninety-minute cycles. Think of each cycle as a "V." Imagine that the top of the "V" on the left side is the point where you place your head on the pillow. You take a moment to think over the day and say your prayers; then Mr. or Ms. Sandman shows up and off to sleep you go. It takes forty-five minutes to float down into the deepest point in your first sleep cycle. If you're awakened while in this deep stage of sleep, you feel disturbed; you may even wake up disoriented. But as soon as you reach this deep phase, you start on your way back up the right side of the "V" toward lighter sleep.

It takes another forty-five minutes to waft upward to the top part of the "V" on the right-hand side. The top of the cycle is the shallowest period of sleep. During this time you dream and you can be easily awakened. When you finish this ninety-minute "V" sleep cycle, you enter a new cycle—down the left-hand side to deep, deep sleep; then up the right-hand side again toward the shallow sleep stage where dreams occur. The cycles recur regularly until you wake up.

How can you use this information to your advantage? That's where the answers to the previous questions come into play. Let's look at your answers in reverse order.

- Take the number of hours you sleep during an average night and divide it by 1.5 (one and one-half hours). If you sleep six hours per night, you sleep in four ninety-minute sleep cycles per night. If you sleep seven and a half hours, then you experience five ninety-minute sleep cycles per night. If a fraction of a cycle is left over after you divide the number of sleep hours by 1.5, then you're waking up somewhere in the midst of the sleep cycle rather than at the end of it, when the body is naturally primed to wake up.

Here's a concrete example. Let's say you go to bed at 11:00 P.M., and your alarm clock is set to go off at 5:30 A.M. That's six and a half hours of sleep, or four cycles and some fraction left over. When your alarm goes off, your body is descending into the deep-sleep phase of a cycle. You will likely wake up groggy rather than bright-eyed and bushy-tailed.

๏ Do you use a snooze alarm? If you answered, "Yes," then your alarm clock is probably set to go off when you're somewhere in the middle of a ninety-minute cycle rather than at the end of one. So, you snooze, snooze, snooze…until you reach a point in your cycle where your body is ready to wake up. Planning your sleep night in multiples of ninety-minute cycles and then setting your alarm accordingly will make your snooze alarm obsolete.

๏ How many hours do you sleep each night? Any answer is, of course, acceptable, but the ideal answer is in multiples of ninety minutes. That means an individual should plan for six hours (four ninety-minute cycles), seven and a half hours (five complete cycles), or nine hours (six cycles) of sleep each night. Health experts have found that seven and a half hours is the amount of sleep most often associated with good health.

๏ Do you awaken alert or groggy? Once again, if you plan your sleep night in complete ninety-minute cycles, you'll wake up ready to go. If you set your clock to wake up somewhere within a cycle, it will be harder to get up and get going. Remember that your children sleep in cycles, too. They'll wake up easier if you rouse them at the end of a sleep cycle.

What's the cheap psychological trick? It's really more physiological than psychological. Plan your sleep night in multiples of ninety-minute cycles and your sleep will be more refreshing, and perhaps your dreams more pleasant. And you just might wake up on the right side of the bed!

REFERENCES
Dement, W. C. *Some Must Watch While Some Must Sleep.* San Francisco: W. H. Freeman, 1974.
"How Much Is Enough? If You're Talking About Sleep." *Psychology Today* May–June (1996): 10.
Kleitman, N. "Patterns of Dreaming." *Scientific American* November (1960): 82–88.

Cheap Trick No. 21

Plates, Patterns, and Pounds – How to Avoid Overeating

T hink back to your childhood days when mom or dad prepared your meals. In addition to begging and pleading, your parents probably used a CPT to persuade you to eat your food.

What did your favorite childhood plate or bowl look like? Was there a figure or a design on the bottom? It may have been Batman, Little Red Riding Hood, or Walt Disney's Dumbo. No matter who it depicted, the figure at the bottom of the plate looking back at you actually influenced your eating—people tend to eat until they can see whatever design is hidden under the food!

What's the cheap psychological trick? If there is a design or pattern on our china, we eat until we can see the design clearly. If you're on a diet, eat from plates with no design—or even better, from plain white china. Without the design present to influence you, you have less incentive to clean your plate.

Other tricks to remember:

- Do not eat from red or yellow plates or dine in establishments with this color decor. When surrounded by red or yellow, we have a tendency to eat faster and more. (Do any fast-food restaurants come to mind?)
- Dine while listening to slower, more relaxing music. The slower tempo will slow your actions, giving your brain more time to receive the message from your stomach that you're full.
- Wait at least five minutes after you finish an entree before you start your dessert. The neural connections between the stomach and the brain are the slowest in the body. As a result, it takes a little extra time for the brain to know that your stomach is full. If you wait a while, you are more likely to decline the sweet ending to the meal.

Bon appetit!

REFERENCES

"How to Stay Slender for Life." *Reader's Digest* 21 (1982): 117.

"Making Weight: Tips for Successful Dieting." *Coach and Athlete* November–December (1981): 25–28.

Cheap Trick No. 22

Condition Yourself

You don't need to know about Pavlov and his dogs to use this cheap psychological trick, but a brief refresher course in this scientist's findings will help you apply this trick with aplomb.

Once upon a time there was a Russian scientist by the name of Ivan Pavlov. He's revered for his documentation of "classical conditioning." Here's a quick rundown of his findings:

- He noticed that when given food, dogs would salivate. (In fact, dogs, just like humans, are wired to salivate to aid digestion.)
- Then he began ringing a bell before each feeding time; he noticed that the dogs began to salivate at the sound of the bell, before he presented their food.
- He rang the bell but provided no food; the dogs still

salivated at the sound of the bell.

◉ The dogs eventually began to salivate when they heard Pavlov's footsteps, in anticipation of the food they expected.

With just a little learning, the animals were conditioned to salivate to the bell and footsteps because they associated those sounds with food; their salivary glands began producing the normal output of saliva to aid with digestion even when no food was offered.

How do the results of Pavlov's studies apply to you? Some allergy sufferers experience symptoms at the mere sight of a flower, but once they realize it's made of silk, the sneezing stops. They are so thoroughly conditioned to sneeze around flowers that a harmless object can trigger an allergic reaction. You can use such conditioning to your advantage by influencing and even conditioning your immune system with this cheap psychological trick.

Researchers discovered the basis for this wonderful trick (*they* call it a statistically significant finding) by accident. They gave rats a drug that would suppress the functioning of the immune system, and the drug organically altered each rat's physiology.

Along with each injection, they gave the rats saccharine-water. After repeated pairings of the sweet water and drug, the sweet water alone was found to produce the same results as the drug! The rats' immune systems were tricked into "thinking" they were receiving the drug. The drug suppressed the immune system; after pairings with the drug, the sweet water alone suppressed the immune system.

Research for application to humans is quite promising in this area, but remember to *make sure* you check with your health-care professional before you try any type of alternative medicine!

What's the cheap psychological trick? Perhaps you take medicine for arthritis pain, and the pills are quite effective in alleviating your discomfort. Try this experiment: Right before you take your pain-relieving pill, sniff your favorite flower (the flower should be noticeably fragrant) or your favorite perfume. According to the laws of classical conditioning, after successive pairings, the fragrance alone could begin to trigger your body's natural painkillers. If you are taking a powerful drug, if your physician has warned you about taking too much of the drug, and if pain tends to set in before it's time for your next dose, this trick might help you. (Check with your physician and always follow directions. Be smart— do not abandon necessary medicine in favor of this method; instead see if you can gradually condition your body to supplement your medication by producing more endorphins.)

Here's another possibility. If you suffer from headaches and are taking a pill that effectively reduces the pain, each time you feel a headache coming on, take your pill with orange juice (assuming your physician approves). Successive pairings may just trick your body into thinking that orange juice eases the pain. The result may be fewer headaches and more vitamin C.

You could even try this trick using music. If you always take your medicine while you're listening to Mozart's "Sonata in C," after repeated pairings, the music itself may do your body good. Choose music with a strong melody and few, if any, words.

REFERENCE

Ader, R., and N. Cohen. "CNS–Immune System Interactions: Conditioning Phenomena." *Behavioral and Brain Sciences* 8 (1985): 379–394.

Cheap Trick No. 23

No More Nasty Habits

Human beings are nail-biting, coughing, denture-clicking, hair-twirling, scratching, foot-tapping, jewelry-fiddling, bead-bumbling, whistling, and gossiping machines. Do you suck on your pens and then stick them in your ears? Do you pull your hair or beard out by the roots? Do you stick your nose in places where it just doesn't belong? Do you bite your nails down past the cuticles? Is your conversation filled with "uhs," "likes," "duhs," and "you knows"?

If your nasty behaviors are bothering you, they are certain to be annoying the people around you. Isn't it about time you made an effort to get rid of your worst habits? You could spend thousands of dollars on psychotherapy to discover why you suck your thumb at age thirty-five, or you could try some cheap psychological tricks that will—if used properly and consistently—stop your nasty habits in their tracks.

What's the cheap psychological trick? Here's the first one: Say you bite your fingernails or tug at your beard. Find a rubber band—not a wimpy one, a first-class one. Place the rubber band around your wrist on your nondominant hand. (If you're right-handed put the rubber band on your left wrist and vice versa.) Here's the hard part. When your hand goes toward your hair or beard or when you put your fingers in your mouth, even when you catch your fingers halfway toward your face, deliver one painful rubber-band pop to your wrist. It takes about three days to stop a nasty habit this way. By then you will probably have a red welt on the wrist. (Use this for yourself; it's not recommended for your children.)

Here's another trick called "negative practice." This doesn't work with nail biting or hair pulling, but it does work with "uhs," "likes," and "you knows." Deliberately repeat your problem words over and over and over until you are totally bored or fatigued by them. For example, suppose your vocabulary is dominated by "uhs" or "ahs" when you are in stressful situations. Take ten to fifteen minutes each day for about three consecutive days and constantly repeat (stopping only to breathe) these pseudowords. They soon will become repugnant to you.

Does your mother-in-law take towels from hotels? Would you like to stop her kleptoid behavior? Try a cheap technique called "flooding" to make her stop. Assuming you visit her regularly, each time you visit take her ten cheap towels. After ten visits she has one hundred towels; twenty visits brings the total to two hundred. She'll get the point, **69** and towels will no longer seem valuable to her. The point is to "flood" the "collector" with his or her obsession so that the excitement of the habit disappears.

REFERENCES

Goldiamond, I. "Fluent and Nonfluent Speech (Stuttering): Analysis and Operant Techniques for Control." *Research in Behavior Modification.* Edited by M. S. Gazzaniga and E. P. Lovejoy. Englewood Cliffs, NJ: Prentice Hall, 1971.

Mahoney, M. J., and C. E. Thorsen. *Self-Control: Power to the Person.* Monterey, CA: Brooks/Cole Publishing Co., 1974.

Mursell, J. L. *How to Make and Break Habits.* New York: J. B. Lippincott Co., 1953.

•••••• 4 ••••••

Re-Cycle Yourself

Cheap Trick No. 24

Working With Your Circadian Clock

You may not know it, but the 24- to 26-hour clock ticking away inside of you is incredibly precise. So precise, in fact, that some researchers suggest that if you were born at four o'clock in the morning, you'll die at four o'clock in the morning. (Assuming death by natural causes, of course. An internal clock is no match for a speeding bus!) It seems that the master body clock *completes* a 24- to 26-hour cycle before it shuts the body down for good.

This physiological clock, set according to 24-hour segments called "circadian" cycles, takes you through each day, but not without some resistance—American culture works against it in many ways. However, working *with* your internal clock requires very little effort on your part, guarantees almost immediate results, and is probably the cheapest psychological or biological trick of all.

Before further explanation, let's see how well you understand and work with your circadian rhythms. Answer the following questions as accurately as possible:

What time of day do you think:

* you are you most apt to pick a fight?
* you feel pain the strongest?
* you are most susceptible to alcohol?
* you should try on clothes?
* you are most prone to accidents?
* you are most accurate doing detail work like proofreading?
* you are at your best for meetings?
* you should ask for a raise?
* you should avoid going to the dentist or doctor?
* your blood pressure is its highest?
* you are most likely to hear "NO"?
* you should take a nap?
* you are at your sexual peak?

Take a look at the following chart for a rundown of an **73**

average person's ideal circadian schedule. Keep in mind that the sun dictates your internal clock; the times listed below will differ according to your time zone. Individual physiology and psychology will also influence your personal circadian clock; for example, introverts tend to have their morning energy peak earlier than extroverts.

W**hat's the cheap psychological trick?** To organize your day for maximum results, follow this chart based on the body's circadian clock and human physiology. Read the following sections for detailed discussions of the circadian cycle.

REFERENCE
Moore-Ede, Martin C., Frank M. Sulzman, and Charles A. Fuller. *The Clocks that Time Us*. Cambridge, MA: Harvard University Press, 1982.

Time Management by Physiology

7:00 A.M.	**WAKING UP**
7:00 – 8:00 A.M.	**GETTING STARTED**
	• Sexual peak
8:00 A.M. – noon	**RELATING TO PEOPLE**
	• Meetings
	• Make and return phone calls
Noon – 1:30 P.M.	**LUNCH BREAK**
	• Susceptibility to alcohol at highest level
1:30 – 2:00 P.M.	**DROP IN HORMONE LEVEL**
	• Naptime, or the "Illusion of Busy" (see CPT No. 27)
2:00 – 5:00 P.M.	**ANALYTICAL TIME**
	• Attend to details
	• Avoid personal interaction, including phone calls
	• Recognize that pain is at its highest level
6:00 – 8:00 P.M.	**EXERCISING AND SPENDING TIME WITH FAMILY**
	• Dinner
10:00 P.M.	**SECOND WIND**
	• If you need it (but don't expect it every night)
11:00 P.M. – 7:00 A.M.	**SLEEP**
	• Least productive time of day.

Cheap Trick No. 25

Your Sexual Peak

*A*s soon as you wake up in the morning, your body begins to create the hormones that will sustain you until about two o'clock in the afternoon. One of the first hormones to kick in triggers the craving for sexual activity. Why is the body set up this way? Scientists think that this particular body mechanism harks back to prehistoric man. Nature drove man to try to perpetuate the species before going out into a very dangerous world where death could occur in the blink of a saber-toothed tiger's eye.

How powerful is this craving for sex in the early morning? Powerful enough to perpetuate the species and allow most people to put aside their personal inhibitions. You've probably noticed that morning radio shows are incredibly ribald, sometimes even vulgar; disc jockeys take great liberties in the early morning drive-time shows, and their speech is often laden with sexual innuendo. Yet radio stations rarely get complaints. Now take this same show and run it at four o'clock in the afternoon, and phones will most likely ring off the hook with complaining listeners. Why? The biological craving for sex is not as intense in the afternoon as it is in early morning. In fact, when an urge or craving is at its highest in the morning, it is at its weakest in the afternoon.

What's the cheap psychological trick? You can use your internal clock to your advantage when it comes to sex by asking for sex in the morning—the person you're with is subject to the same awakening hormones. (Try sex in the morning if you are having trouble "performing"; your body will be working with you instead of making your mind do all the work!)

REFERENCE
Moore-Ede, Martin C., Frank M. Sulzman, and Charles A. Fuller. *The Clocks that Time Us.* Cambridge, MA: Harvard University Press, 1982.

Cheap Trick No. 26

The Morning Rush

rom about 5:00 A.M. until about 8:00 A.M., your body generates the chemicals necessary to get you up and going. For most people, the most productive time of day begins around 8:00 A.M. and lasts until noon. This is a "people time of day," when we want to listen and understand, are more likely to agree with one another, and are willing to compromise. Move your meeting to the afternoon, when the body is no longer craving these associations, and your encounters will run longer, get tangled up in trivial detail, and run into increased questioning and irritability. Remember the eight- to twelve-hour rule—when an urge or skill is at its strongest at a certain time of day, it will be at its weakest eight to twelve hours later.

There are some psychological twists to this "people time of day." If you are an introvert, you will tend to peak earlier in the day; in fact, people who prefer to work alone rather than in groups of people are most energized and efficient between 8:00 A.M. and 10:00 A.M. Extroverts, those who love people and talk constantly, find their most productive time of day to be between 10:00 A.M. and noon. Almost as interesting as this statistic is the fact that scientists don't really know why introverts and extroverts peak at different times!

What's the cheap psychological trick? People—introverted or extroverted—are more productive and more positive in the mornings.

* Want a raise? Plan a meeting with your supervisor in the morning, when he or she is more likely to listen and even agree with you.
* Showing real-estate? Morning shows are more productive than afternoon ones.
* Want a person to sign a contract? Morning meetings are the best. Afternoons are for other things. (Keep reading!)

REFERENCE

Moore-Ede, Martin C., Frank M. Sulzman, and Charles A. Fuller. *The Clocks that Time Us.* Cambridge, MA: Harvard University Press, 1982.

Cheap Trick No. 21

Two Martinis and a Nap

*L*unchtime! You made it through the morning, now it's time for the ritual called "lunch." You're probably starving and ready to wolf down whatever is available. Well, that's your body's way of saying, "You've waited too long to feed me!" Research has shown that people perform more productively and feel better when they eat four or five small meals a day rather than three large ones. In fact, having only three meals a day is a relatively new cultural convention. Small meals equally spaced throughout the day keep the digestive system working slower and more rhythmically, whereas large meals require the same system to work harder for brief periods, then to lie idle for long stretches. But most of us follow the schedules society imposes on us; we eat a big lunch around noon.

After lunch you may notice that you "don't have the

energy to cuss a cat" (to quote my grandmother). This time of day is called the "postprandial dip." Many people believe that the after-lunch sluggishness is a result of the digestion process. Although this theory may be true in part, your drowsiness is due primarily to a depletion of bodily chemicals. All the chemicals your body manufactured to get you up and going in the morning are now used up, and your body needs to take a little time out to create more hormones to get you through the rest of the day. Also keep in mind that your body is most susceptible to alcohol during the postprandial dip. A two-martini lunch will only further depress your system as it naturally slows down in the early afternoon. If you have to go back to the office, alcohol at lunch is only going to slow you down.

How can you best deal with postprandial slump? Take a nap. You have fewer body chemicals to work with during this dip; your productivity is likely to suffer, so you might as well take a nap. If you think naptime would never go over at your workplace, you're wrong. Those who go back to their desks and work through their slumps are probably napping, but in a slightly **81** different way. They may try to look busy straightening their desks, tying up loose ends, etc., but they are actually allowing their bodies to recoup those essential chemicals. This phenomenon of corporate America is called the "illusion of busy." Many other cultures recognize the biology of this time of day and extend the lunch hour to two or more hours or close for "siesta."

Here are three ways to tackle postprandial dip:

* Eat small meals throughout the day to keep your system working at a more constant level.
* Eat a big lunch and take a nap.
* Eat a big lunch and do easy jobs for about an hour after you return to the office.

What's the cheap psychological trick? Your body will slow down no matter what you do, so take advantage of the mental and physical downtime.

REFERENCES

Kukorelli, T., and G. Juhasz. "Sleep Induced by Intestinal Stimulation in Cats." *Physiological Behavior* 19 (1977): 355–358.

Moore-Ede, Martin C., Frank M. Sulzman, and Charles A. Fuller. *The Clocks that Time Us.* Cambridge, MA: Harvard University Press, 1982.

Cheap Trick No. 28

Bite Me!

Now that you have survived your postprandial dip, you must deal with the rest of the afternoon. You've got a new set of chemicals and cravings to get you through it. But unlike the morning chemicals that jump-start your system after a night of rest, the afternoon chemicals make you unsociable and irritable. This is the time of day when you ask a simple question and get your head bitten off. In fact, hospital personnel treat more human bites during this time of day than any other.

The best thing you can do for yourself while these chemicals are busy in your system is to avoid people and catch up on your paperwork. If you have things to proofread—a contract, a letter, a memo—do it now. You'll be surprised at the number of errors you'll catch and the corrections you'll make during this analytic time of day. If you return phone calls at around 4:00 in the afternoon—like most people—you are flying in the face of circadian clock wisdom. If there is a "no" to be said, you are guaranteed to hear it quicker and louder now. *This is the wrong time of day to relate to anyone!*

This is also the time of day when pains are most intense. Patients often feel worse in the late afternoon, and fevers sometimes spike. (Although pain is strongest now, it diminishes to its lowest point in the early morning hours, allowing the body to get much-needed sleep.)

W**hat's the cheap psychological trick?** Use your afternoons well with these helpful hints to guide you:

* Need to return phone calls? Do your dialing in the morning rather than the late afternoon. Your conversations will be more productive and pleasant, and the chances of getting a "yes" are much greater.
* Need to fire someone? Do it in the afternoon. Because your physiology is primed for a fight, it will be easier for you to be ruthless.
* Looking for a job? Avoid afternoon appointments for job interviews. Interviewers will be far less critical during the morning hours.
* Need a dentist? Unless you must, don't schedule a late-afternoon appointment. The drill seems louder and hurts more at this time of day. For the same reasons, avoid physicians in the late afternoon when you are physiologically primed to wince at each poke and prod.
* Did your child misbehave this afternoon? Delay punishment until you get these nasty hormones out of your

system. Count to ten; better yet, count ten hours, letting the cycle run its course, and then punish if you still think it is necessary.

* Craving happy hour at the local bar? Ever wondered why they don't have happy hours in the early morning? Most people don't crave the depressant alcohol before noon. The craving kicks in for many as the hormonal stresses and strains felt in the late afternoon build up—it's a misguided attempt at self-medication. (A movie or a walk would be a great deal healthier.)

* Got a lot of pent-up emotional energy, even anger? See your mental health professional late in the day. You'll "abreact," "cathart," "spill your guts," and deal with emotional topics easier at this time of day. You're primed physiologically to hurt "better" after 4:00 P.M.

* Need to make a large purchase? This is a great time to do your research before you buy. You will be more critical, analytical, and practical, and you'll be more difficult to please. If you postpone your shopping trip until late in the afternoon, you won't buy as much. It takes a lot to make a person happy at 4:00 P.M.!

REFERENCE

Moore-Ede, Martin C., Frank M. Sulzman, and Charles A. Fuller. *The Clocks that Time Us.* Cambridge, MA: Harvard University Press, 1982.

Cheap Trick No. 29

Home By Five

You've made it through the eight-to-five grind, but the irritability of the afternoon is not totally out of your system. So when your loving spouse says, "How was your day?" you may be tempted to snap, punch, or yell. Use this trick instead: Exercise. (Some sources say your body benefits more from a workout at this time of day than any other.)

Unfortunately, while your body may be ready for a run, your brain is ready to settle in and watch the evening news. Not only are you craving food at this time of day, but you're also probably craving some of the blood, guts, and gore of the news. In fact, many people deal with their irritability by watching the bad things that happened to good people during the day.

This is also the fattest time of day, because your body

has worked hard to store all the nutrients it needs to get it through the next day. So, if you need a new pair of shoes, now is a great time to try them on. If they're a perfect fit to-night, they'll feel even better tomorrow morning.

After dinner and exercise your body will begin to slow down in preparation for the evening's rest. Respiration slows down as you sleep. By the wee hours of the morning, around 3:00 or 4:00 A.M., pains are hardly felt at all, blood pressure is at its lowest, and the digestive process takes a little nap, too. The very early morning hours are also the worst possible time to use heavy equipment. If you must drive between midnight and 6:00 A.M., slow down and keep yourself alert. The brain and body just don't work as efficiently at this time of day.

What's the cheap psychological trick? Don't let the irritability of the afternoon ruin your evenings. Recognize the natural slowing process your body goes through during the night and you will work with, rather than against, your circadian clock.

REFERENCE
Moore-Ede, Martin C., Frank M. Sulzman, and Charles A. Fuller. *The Clocks that Time Us.* Cambridge, MA: Harvard University Press, 1982.

·····5·····

Just Between Me and Thee

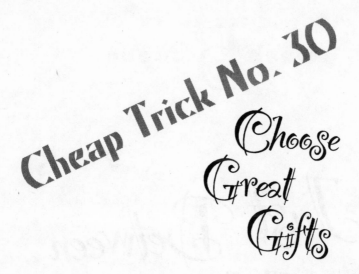

Cheap Trick No. 30

Choose Great Gifts

id you know that 40 percent of the gifts you give will be disliked by the person for whom the gift is intended? That means that two out of every five gifts will likely be thrown in a closet never to be used (or to be recycled by the recipient the next time they need to buy a gift for someone).

Would you like to be able to predict in advance that the gift you give will be appreciated? There is a way to increase your odds of choosing an appropriate gift, and of course, it's a CPT.

It's as simple as something called the "attribution theory." By nature, we tend to judge others' actions and assume their behavior is caused by some general personality characteristic. However, when we judge our own behaviors, we rarely blame our personality; instead, we blame something physical, environmental, or situational. If someone is late to meet you, you might automatically consider the person irresponsible or unreliable, but if you are running late to meet someone else, you might account for your tardiness by noting that your child was ill and the babysitter was difficult to reach.

How can this theory explain something as simple as gift giving? Easily.

Most people select gifts based on their assessment of another person's personality, and it is difficult to translate these appraisals into gifts. If your best friend Bob's personality is outgoing and fun-loving, you may be tempted to buy him an outrageous gift. However, remember that personality is not automatically the best clue to choosing appropriate presents. A better, safer bet is to select a gift based on what the person likes to do. If you take the time to consider someone's activities and choose a gift accordingly, the recipient will be more likely to use or cherish the gift.

For example, do you have a friend who dotes on a dog or a cat? That person probably spends a great deal of time and energy caring for that pet, and that's an action of which you can take note. Buy a toy for the pet or a frame for a photo of the pet, and you can be reasonably sure that your gift won't languish in a drawer somewhere.

Does your friend or colleague enjoy an activity for which you could purchase accessories? You could supply tees, balls, or other golf toys for a golfing friend. Remember, people enjoy receiving presents related to their favorite pastimes.

Do you have an accountant friend who turns into a music aficionado at night? You could buy him or her something conservative to match that careful, steady personality, or a set of fine pens to use at work, but wouldn't it be a better idea to give a CD, a concert ticket, or a set of blank tapes to record the music he or she loves?

What's the cheap psychological trick? If you want to give your friends pleasing and exciting gifts, pay attention to actions more than personality, and select items related to what they enjoy doing.

REFERENCES

Heider, F. *The Psychology of Interpersonal Relations.* New York: Wiley, 1958.

Rice, B. "Performance Review: The Job Nobody Likes." *Psychology Today* September (1985): 30–36.

Storms, M. D. "Videotape and the Attribution Process. Reversing Actors' and Observers' Points of View." *Journal of Personality and Social Psychology* 27 (1973): 165–175.

Cheap Trick No. 31

What You Say Is What They Do

Unfortunately, it's a quirk of psychological nature that we tend to remember the negatives in life a lot longer than we remember the positives. The technical name for this phenomenon is the "Zeigarnik Effect." Simply stated, it means that we not only remember negative feelings and experiences longer than positive ones, but we also feel a greater impact from negative messages than we do from positive ones.

If you want a child to have a more positive attitude, you must consistently accentuate positives and avoid introducing negativity. How? It's a cheap psychological trick, and it has more to do with what you say than with what you do.

Here are some examples. Consider how often you have said things like this to your child:

"Take this glass of milk, and don't spill it."

"Don't slam the door."

"Study hard so you don't fail the test."

After saying such things, have you noticed that the glass spills, the door slams, and the student fails? You may think your child is being deliberately disobedient, but if your child is fairly young, there may be something else going on entirely.

In order to mentally process your commands, young children follow in their heads the scenario you have presented to them, right down to the negative ending you warned against. The child who is told not to spill the glass of milk must focus on the milk spilling. Keep in mind that children do not have the mental faculties to take in what you have said without first "seeing" your statement in their minds; learn to state your commands or warnings positively and ward off those negative results.

For instance, look at the phrases above reworded to create a positive mental picture in the child's mind rather than a negative one.

"Take this milk and hold it with both hands."

"Close the door gently."

"Study hard, and you'll do well on the test."

Of course, teaching children straightforward negative consequences is valuable in some instances. For example, when explaining safety issues, such as electrical outlets and their dangers, or the necessity of looking both ways when crossing the road, the physical harm and consequences of disobeying your advice should be clearly outlined.

What's the cheap psychological trick? Make a conscious effort to present positive, helpful remind-
ers to your child. The messages you send to your children
directly affect their actions.

Use this trick when you are working with adults, too.
Some of us still haven't developed sufficient mental capacities to avoid acting out negative suggestions, and some of us
simply prefer "prescription" to "proscription."

REFERENCE

Zeigarnik, B. "Uber das Behalten von Erledigten und Unerledigten Handlungen." *Psychologische Forschung* 9
(1927): 1–85.

Cheap Trick No. 32

Get to the Root of Anger

Here's a trick question that has a trick answer. How many emotions are there? One researcher has listed as many as 750 emotions. But in a general sense, emotions can be divided into three groups: positive ones, negative ones, and neutral ones. Simply stated, most emotions are really thoughts that make you feel good, bad, or neutral. For example, inferiority is not an emotion—it's a thought that makes you feel bad about yourself. Even love fits in here. Sometimes when you're in love, you feel great and lousy at the same time. If you fall out of love, you go back to neutral.

One secondary emotion, however, is a bit tricky: anger. Anger is a cover-up emotion; it masks what is really going on. When people are angry, they usually let you know it. They may rant and rave, fume and pout in silence, or slam doors.

No matter the form of expression, the CPT should follow this first burst of anger.

What's the cheap psychological trick? Instead of yelling back or clamming up, always ask, "What's the matter?" Most people will tell you something without hesitation. Allow them to spew the requisite venom and calm themselves. Anything you do while they're in this initial phase of anger will only exacerbate the problem, so just listen to what they say.

When they have calmed down, ask them, "Is there anything else that's bothering you?" Anger is always a cover-up emotion protecting the individual. What they answer the first time you ask "What's wrong?" is often a relatively easy topic for them to discuss, usually related to a recent event (the proverbial straw that broke the camel's back). Their *second* response is

I say, is there anything else bothering you?

more likely to reveal a deeper, more important hurt or concern. Asking the right questions can help you turn anger into conversation and deal with others more effectively.

REFERENCES

Berkowitz, L. "On the Formation and Regulation of Anger and Aggression: A Congnitive-Neoassociationistic Analysis." *American Psychologist* 45 (1990): 494–503.

Markus, H., and S. Kitayama. "Culture and the Self: Implications for Cognition, Emotion, and Motivation. *Psychological Review* 98 (1991): 224–253.

Tavris, C. "Anger Defused." *Psychology Today* November (1982): 25–35.

Cheap Trick No. 33

How to Say No

Have trouble with people who just won't give up until they get what they want? Most employees and parents of adolescents are familiar with this frustrating situation. The next time you just can't get the petitioners to give up (and shut up!), try the "broken record" trick. Say your sixteen-year-old wants to go to an unsupervised dance where you have reason to believe alcohol will be flowing in abundance. When your sweet sixteen says, "May I go?" you answer, "I'm sorry, you can't go." If your mind is made up, stick to the script and stay calm.

Adolescent: "But Mom (or Dad), everyone will be there."

Adult: "No, you may not go to the dance tonight."

Adolescent: "I'll be in by eleven."

Adult: "No, you may not go to the dance tonight."

Adolescent: "All of my friends will be there."

Adult: "No, you may not go to the dance tonight."

Adolescent: (volume escalates) "I can't believe you're treating me this way!"

Adult: (calm and collected) "No, you may not go to the dance tonight."

Adolescent: (even louder) "Everybody will laugh at me if I don't show up!"

Adult: (even calmer and collected) "No, you may not go to the dance tonight."

Adolescent: (screaming, dispensing the ultimate weapon) "I hate you!"

Adult: (cool as a cucumber) "No, you may not go to the dance tonight."

Adolescent: (storms off in a huff)

The broken-record technique is simple—just repeat the same phrase as often as necessary. The only difficult part of this trick is that you *cannot* raise your voice at any time. When you raise your voice, you let the other person know that you are affected by their tactics, thereby giving up some of your control and authority. This is not the time to offer excuses or explanations—they will only prolong the exchange.

Here's another example. Your boss wants you to work on Saturday, and although you've said, "No," the guilt trip continues. State your position with "No, I can't work, I've got family responsibilities," then use the broken-record method to convince your boss that you mean what you say.

If relatives try to impose their wills on you inappropriately, use the same tactic. Saying, "Mother, I'd rather do it myself," repeatedly *will* eventually convince her that you're not giving in.

An added bonus: this CPT does not rely on or teach aggression as a way to reach your goals. Instead, it shows that you can take a stand and keep it assertively without losing your temper. (It will also show others that you are no longer taking guilt trips!)

Need to refuse someone a favor without offending? Try the three-step empathy response. Say a good friend wants to borrow your car, and it's not an emergency. It is your policy not to loan your car to anyone. To handle this situation, follow these three steps:

- Say, "I know you need a car." (This statement lets your friend know you understand the request.)
- Add, "I'm sorry, but I don't loan out my car." (This statement lets your friend know your position.)
- Finish off with a viable alternative, like, "Can I call you a cab or give you a ride?" (This lets your friend know you're willing to help, which, of course, is the mark of a true friend!)

What are the cheap psychological tricks? Use the broken-record technique and three-step empathy trick, and you'll walk away from conflicts knowing you assertively stood up for your rights and kept your integrity intact.

REFERENCES

Alberti, R., and M. Emmons. *Your Perfect Right.* San Luis Obispo, CA: Impact Publications, 1978.

Carson, R. C., J. N. Butcher, and S. Mineka. *Abnormal Psychology and Modern Life.* New York: HarperCollins, 1996.

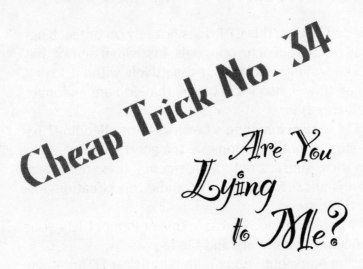

Cheap Trick No. 34

Are You Lying to Me?

Over the years, social scientists have compiled a list of characteristics associated with lying. This list is not 100 percent guaranteed to pick out every liar, but it can help you spot the ones who are lying through their teeth!

The following cheap psychological tricks are based on the social scientists' list and on the Freudian belief that most liars feel a little bad about their deception. The twinges of guilt result in physiological clues to the deception!

Here's what to look for:

- Liars' voices become higher pitched when they are trying to hoodwink a mark.
- Liars gesticulate very little. Few hand motions from persons who like to use their hands is a dead giveaway that they are hiding the truth.

- Liars sound distant when making things up and usually offer little descriptive phrasing. For example, a liar might describe an object as "red," rather than "fire-engine red."
- Liars are more likely to stumble over words or stammer.
- Liars frequently blink, scratch, or bite their nails. Of these three, watch for blinking, especially among political candidates.

Combine these characteristics with the telltale look of panic that bad liars often exhibit when they think they've been caught, and you have some pretty good clues to look out for. (Shifty eyes, slow speech, lengthy pauses before answering questions, shifts in posture, and absence of smiles, once thought to be signs of lying, are not really reliable prevarication predictors.)

What's the cheap psychological trick? Watch carefully, and liars will provide you with physiological clues to their dishonesty. And that's no lie!

REFERENCES

Adler, V. "Lying Smiles." *Psychology Today* July–August (1988): 16.

Carey, B. "What Gives Liars Away." *In Health* January (1990): 30–33.

Carey, B. "Do You Know When You've Been Duped?" *Health* July–August (1992): 33.

Cheap Trick No. 35

Potty Train
your
Little Boy

Potty training children can be *very* difficult. As a general rule, little girls are easier to train than little boys, primarily because there is less aiming involved. Sometimes parents need to get creative to get boys to "hit the target." As sure as big boys like to write their names in fresh snow, these CPTs will help make potty training boys more fun and more successful.

Most children like toys that make noise, so why not make the potty trip noisy to pique the child's interest? Try this time-honored trick—float a tin pie pan in the toilet bowl. Have dad demonstrate what happens when the urine splatters on the pan—it creates quite a clatter!—and the child will double over in giggles. He will very likely follow dad's lead and give the toilet a try.

If the charm of this technique wears off, put little paper

boats in the (preferably blue) toilet water, and ask the child to move the boats around—but without using his hands. Once again, dad makes a great model for this technique. (Unless you have exceptional plumbing or water-soluble boats, you may want to hold off teaching the child to flush until a later session!) If boats seem too elaborate, try a small amount of a buoyant cereal like Cheerios or Froot-Loops—cereal flushes quite easily!

Finally, you can give the child a target. With bathtub paint, draw an X, a bull's-eye, or a red dot where the urine should be directed.

What's the cheap psychological trick? Give your little boy an incentive that he'll enjoy. Whatever the target, your child will better his technique and have fun at the same time. Some hearty praise and perhaps a little reward for your straight-shooter when he hits the mark will reinforce the "targeted" behavior.

REFERENCE
Dr. Buff's grandma.

Cheap Trick No. 36

Get a Secret Out of Someone

Probably every child has teased a classmate with the singsong taunt, "I know something you don't know!" Remember how those words drove you crazy when you were a child? If only you had known a surefire method of making others talk! In fact, there *is* a way (without introducing methods of torture) to make even the most secretive people tell all!

What's the cheap psychological trick? There are actually several tricks you can try. The first is an old reporter's trick of asking a question and waiting. Sometimes the extended silence is uncomfortable enough that the other person feels compelled to say something. Adding a leveled stare can also help.

106   If the person still refuses to tell the secret, say things

like, "Give me a hint," or "Let me guess it." Teasing the secret out of them makes it all a game; in a playful atmosphere, the other person may let down his or her guard and confide in you.

One important caveat: Never beg to hear a secret. When you beg, you give the person with the secret the upper hand in the situation. Pleading shows the other person that you desperately want to know and reminds them that they can remain in control by keeping you in the dark. Instead, turn the tables and act indifferent and uninterested; your friend will become concerned with having (and sharing) information you'll find intriguing.

One other trick involves sharing information of your own. Tell something juicy about yourself, and other people will often feel compelled to continue the volley of gossip. When they share something about themselves, add something even juicier (it's like tossing in another poker chip). They'll probably raise the stakes with more information. When you get them talking, ask, "Now, really, what was that secret?" In light of all you've shared with each other, keeping the secret becomes less important and they'll be more likely to share it.

Remember, once you perfect these techniques, don't divulge how they are done. Keep them a secret or your friends will never tell you another thing!

REFERENCES

Bandura, A. *Social Foundations of Thought and Action.* Englewood Cliffs, NJ: Prentice-Hall, 1986.
Seedman, A. "Best Way to Spill the Beans." *Redbook* December (1994).

Mind Over Matter

Cheap Trick No. 31

Lighten Your Load

Too many gray-sky days in a row can really make you sad and make you suffer from a condition called SAD—Seasonal Affect Disorder. As many as one in every five people may suffer from SAD.

If you fear you may be suffering from this disorder, first contact a health-care professional. He or she may recommend changing at least one light bulb in a fixture at home to full-spectrum lighting. You can do this by installing a special light bulb that creates the full array of colors present in natural light. The body interprets full-spectrum light the same way it interprets sunlight, so that in most cases, using this special bright light (which is ten to fifteen times brighter than regular indoor light) for fifteen to thirty minutes a day can send the winter blahs on their way. These

lighting systems are particularly effective at reducing the

number of gray-day, cabin-fever, winter-depression symptoms.

What's the cheap psychological trick? If you think you may suffer from this problem, first get approval from your physician (my attorney continually makes me say that), then change your light bulb to a full-spectrum light. You can obtain one at many light stores, or you can order directly from The SunBox Company, 19217 Orbit Drive, Gaithersburg, Maryland 20879 (800-548-3968). Believe it or not, many insurance policies will pay for this equipment. For more information on SAD, call the "Winter Blues Resource Service" (800-FIX-BLUEs).

Don't be sad—use a CPT and become en-light-ened!

REFERENCES

Cunningham, M. R. "Weather, Mood, and Helping Behavior." *Journal of Personality and Social Psychology* 37 (1979): 1947–1956.

Rosenthal, N. E., D. A. Sack, J. C. Gillin, A. J. Lewry, F. K. Goodwin, Y. Davenport, P. S. Mueller, D. A. Newsome, and T. A. Wehr. "Seasonal Affective Disorder: A Description of the Syndrome and Preliminary Findings with Light Therapy." *Archives of General Psychiatry* 41 (1984): 72–80.

Wehr T. A., F. M. Jacobsen, D. A. Sack, J. Arendt, L. Tamarkin, N. E. Rosenthal, "Phototherapy of Seasonal Affective Disorder." *Archives of General Psychiatry* 43 (1986): 870–875.

Cheap Trick No. 38

No Pain, All Gain – Mental Practice and Success

What does it take to be the top salesperson, the fastest typist, the finest manager, the best doctor, a spectacular parent, or the gold-medal winner in a sports event? There is one technique that appears to be foolproof, and it's found right inside your head. It's the power of your very own thoughts. As nonscientific as it sounds, empirical, sophisticated research has shown that the way people think can separate champions from also-rans. This way of thinking is known simply as "mental rehearsal." Here's how to rehearse mentally:

🍂 Be accurate in your rehearsal. You've heard the old expression, "Practice makes perfect." Not quite. Any practice, including mental practice, makes *permanent*, not perfect. If you practice incorrectly, it will adversely affect your physical performance. Work out an accurate step-by-step sequence of behaviors that you can mentally rehearse. They must be consistent with the actual physical behavior; otherwise, you are sabotaging your own work. Write the steps down and carry the list with you. During each day, take it out, read it, and mentally rehearse the steps.

🌱 As you mentally rehearse, give yourself a positive, "I know I can do it" pep talk. If your mental rehearsal takes on a pessimistic tone, this negative outlook will carry over to the actual event. If you think optimistically while you are mentally rehearsing, the positive approach will show through in your physical performance.

🌱 Choose the right time of day to mentally rehearse. If you are preparing for a physical activity and you cannot physically practice for it, mentally practice at about the same time that the real competition will occur. If you are giving a speech, you can mentally rehearse anytime, but be sure and picture yourself performing admirably at the time of day when the speech will actually be delivered. Prepare your mind to prepare your body.

What's the cheap psychological trick? Mental practice increases the odds of success. Use your mind to influence the outcome of your efforts.

REFERENCES
Seligman, M. E. P. *Helplessness*. New York: Scribner's Sons, 1975.
Seligman, M. E. P. *Learned Optimism*. New York: Knopf, 1991.

Cheap Trick No. 39

The Brain Workout

The story goes that every single day at about 4:00 P.M., a deceptively doddery-looking gray-haired gentleman made his way out of his house and walked toward the local swimming hole. As regular as clockwork, he paused just long enough to ask the neighborhood children about the water, the fishing, and their school work. Then he sauntered on down the path.

Chances are this man knew about a CPT. In fact, Albert Einstein's afternoon constitutional was more than just a walk to the swimming hole. He was probably using his exercise time as an aid for problem-solving.

This is nothing new. Creative people have known for years that a link exists between exercising and solving problems. Charles Dickens organized the plot twists of his novels while zigzagging through the streets of London. Frank Lloyd Wright concocted landmark designs while taking his short walks. Cardinal Richelieu, prime minister of France under Louis XIII, vaulted over furniture as a way of tackling insurmountable problems.

Recall the last time you were stressed out, worried, and confused about a difficult situation. Remember how you found yourself furiously mopping the floors or scrubbing the windows? Then while you were mopping away, a solution to your problem popped into your head—you suddenly knew what to do! Physical activity (which takes your mind off your problem, even for a brief moment) can produce a flash of insight. Einstein said he often had his best ideas during his shaving time every morning. The research in this area is not definitive, but it does appear that any form of exercising (even shaving) can enhance creative problem solving.

Exercise appears to improve problem-solving abilities in another way. Studies at the University of Illinois suggest that exercise increases the number of blood vessels nourishing the brain. After four weeks of aerobic exercise, white rats averaged a 20-percent increase in the number of blood vessels servicing their brains. The extra nourishment improved the speed of brain activity.

What's the cheap psychological trick? When you face a difficult problem that requires some creative worrying, here's what to do:

- Go over the problem in your mind.
- Begin exercise.
- Think about the problem, but don't force a solution.

🌱 After a short time spent thinking about your dilemma, store it away in the back of your brain.

🌱 Think about something else—vacations you would like to take, good books you have read, anything that will keep your mind distracted.

🌱 If the initial problem pops into your head, think about it, refrain from forcing a solution, then stick it in the back of your consciousness again.

🌱 Repeat steps as needed.

🌱 When solutions pop into your head, take them seriously and weigh the pros and cons.

With a little help our overburdened brains can operate just as they are designed, efficiently providing answers and directions to our most puzzling problems. People who exercise also gain much more than added brain nourishment; they give themselves a mental health break, they quiet their minds, and they escape the burdens of the day—at least for a little while.

REFERENCES
"Bulk Up Your Brain." *Men's Health* June (1991): 26.
"Brain Health: Pressure to Perform." *Psychology Today* March–April (1996):16.

Cheap Trick No. 40

The Power of Perspective

*A*s you probably know, the right side of your brain governs the left side of your body, while the left side of the brain governs the right side of your body. The left side of the brain is the spatial, analytical, critical, word-using side for most people. The right side is thought to be less critical, more emotional, even more persuasive. The fact that the right side of the brain is much less judgmental forms the foundation of this cheap psychological trick.

Try this experiment on yourself. Add 525 and 327 in your head. Without your being aware of it, your eyes looked up to the right, a sign that you are engaging your brain in a critical-thinking, analytical task. Think about someone or something you love and your eyes will look up to the left.

Use your knowledge of the different orientations of the brain to help you make a good impression on people. Learn how to engage the side of people's brains that will best suit your purposes.

🌱 Do you have a presentation to make before an audience? Start your presentation from the audience's left so that they will have to turn their eyes to the left, and slowly work your way across the stage to their middle. If you want your listeners to analyze a problem, present it from the audience's right. These simple stage directions will help keep the attention of the audience on you.

🌱 Meeting a blind date for the first time? Try to angle yourself so that you are presented to new acquaintances from their left so that you engage the less critical side of their brains.

🌱 Taking a math or science course? Sit so that you must look to the right to see the instructor. Doing so will engage the part of the brain better able to learn spatial skills. Conversely, if you are taking a music or art appreciation course, sit where you must orient your eyes to the left; you'll engage the part of your brain better able to process this creative material.

🌱 Afraid you will lose your composure at a funeral? Sit where you must look more to the right. You are more likely to keep your emotions under control in this position because your are engaging the more analytical side of your brain.

What's the cheap psychological trick? View things so that you are looking to the left and you will perceive them with a less-critical eye. View things so that you are looking to the right, and you will be much more critical of anything you view. Place yourself in the sights of others according to your needs.

REFERENCES

Davidson, R. J., P. Ekman, C. D. Saron, J. S. Senulis, and W. V. Friesen. "Approach-Withdrawal and Cerebral Asymmetry: Emotional Expression and Brain Physiology." *Journal of Personality and Social Psychology* 58 (1990): 330–341.

Gazzaniga, M. S. *Mind Matters: How Mind and Brain Interact to Create our Conscious Lives.* Boston: Houghton Mifflin, 1988.

Sperry, R. W. "Some Effects of Disconnecting the Cerebral Hemispheres." *Science* 217 (1985): 1223–1226.

Cheap Trick No. 41

Why You Shouldn't Watch the News

*A*re you beginning to believe that the entire world is going to hell in a handbasket? Are you becoming more and more mortified at the current state of affairs, perhaps even afraid to venture out of the house? If the violence, despair, and chaos of the world are getting to you, it may be time to change the way you watch the evening news. With this cheap trick you'll stay informed, but you'll avoid the blood and gore of television news.

What's the cheap psychological trick? *Just don't watch.* Seventy percent of all your sensory intake is visual. The trick is to avoid *seeing* the news, not to avoid the news altogether.

Instead of watching the news, listen to it. *Hearing* about a tragedy does not have the same impact as *seeing* it depicted

graphically on television. Radio news tends to be shorter, more terse, and less likely to suffer from the emotional sensationalism inherent in television programs battling for ratings. If you can't give up your favorite anchorperson, then turn the television on, turn the volume up, but don't watch; avoid the visual stimulation by going to another room or sitting with your back to the set.

Another option is *reading* the news. The written word does not have the emotional impact of a visual demonstration. When you read the newspaper, you can stop, shift topics, skim, and otherwise manipulate the information.

If you read or listen to the news rather than watch it, you'll be better able to assimilate the information, maintain your objectivity, and feel in control.

REFERENCES

Lull, J., ed. *World Families Watch Television.* Newbury Park, CA: Sage, 1996.

Radecki, T. "On Picking Good Television and Film Entertainment." *NCTV News* February–March (1989): 5.

Cheap Trick No. 42

Training to Win

Y ou're training hard for the upcoming race. You've put in the hours, the sweat, the extra strength training. Good for you! There's just one more technique you need to know about, and it can make an outstanding athlete out of a good one. And believe it or not, it requires no special equipment and no physical exertion. People work hard at training themselves physically, but they usually ignore mental training.

W hat's the cheap psychological trick? Get in the habit of using the following CPTs before every big race—you should soon see an improvement.

🎈 The night before the big run, do something to take your mind off the race. Rent a movie, go to a concert, or read a good book—do anything that will distract your mind from the next day's competition.

☂ Plan something exciting to do *after* the race. This is very important. If you're looking forward to something special after the event, you will have more incentive to run well.

☂ As you start the run, count down the number of race miles left to go in reverse order. Most people begin with mile one and count up—mile two, mile three, mile four. A way of tricking your brain into thinking your body has less work left to do is to count backwards. Start with mile six, and count down—mile five, mile four, mile three, mile two. The closer you get to zero, the faster you'll run.

☂ Don't forget the value of mental rehearsal (See CPT No. 38). Mentally practice the run for the same amount of time it will take to physically run the race. You may be sitting in your office, but if the race starts at nine o'clock in the morning, take some time out from work, envision yourself running the race, and visualize doing it faster. After all, in your head, any race can be won.

REFERENCES

Premack, D. "Reinforcement Theory." Edited by M. R. Jones. *Nebraska Symposium on Motivation.* Lincoln: University of Nebraska Press, 1965.

"The Power of Average Thinking." *Longevity* March (1989):26.

"Peak Performance: I Think I Can, I Think I Can." *Psychology Today* March–April (1996): 10.

Cheap Trick No. 43

You are Getting Sleepy . . . .

How did you sleep last night? Estimates show that between 40 and 46 percent of Americans experience some kind of sleep disturbance at some time in their lives. Many of us have difficulty getting to sleep in the first place. We all have our own sleep-inducing rituals—everything from counting sheep to drinking warm milk.

Here's a cheap psychological trick that can help you if you are "slumber challenged." When you rest your head on your pillow at night, instead of worrying about trying to go to sleep, try *to stay awake*. That's right. The act of trying to stay awake as long as you can takes your mind off the worry that you won't be able to get to sleep. The technical name for this is "paradoxical intention." This means that trying to do the *opposite* of what you want can actually help you achieve it.

What's the cheap psychological trick? When you go to bed tonight, don't dare go to sleep. Try to stay awake as long as you can, concentrating only on staying awake. Try not to fall asleep, but don't get out of the bed, either. You'll be amazed at what a good night's sleep you'll finally get!

REFERENCES

Asher, L. M., and J. S. Efran. "Use of Paradoxical Intention in a Behavioral Program for Sleep Onset Insomnia." *Journal of Consulting and Clinical Psychology* 46 (1978): 547–550.

Frankl, V. E. "Paradoxical Intention and Dereflection." *Psychotherapy: Theory, Research, and Practice* 12 (1975): 226–236.

Ghadban, R. "Paradoxical Intention." *Psychological Interventions: A Guide to Strategies.* Edited by Mary Ballou. Westport, CT: Praeger Publishers/Greenwood Publishing Group, 1995.

Cheap Trick No. 44

Rainy Days and Mondays

It's said that rainy days and Mondays always get us down, but the truth is that any period of gloomy, gray days can make us sad and blue. For many people, however, one cheap psychological trick will shed a little "light" on the issue.

Here's how light works on human beings. Light enters the eyes, reaches the brain, and acts directly on those areas that regulate sleep, sex drive, appetite, and mood. During long periods of darkness, the brain calls for the release of the hormone melatonin into your body, and this makes the body feel tired.

Most people—including scientists and other researchers—are in the dark when it comes to a full explanation of how our bodies process and utilize light. One thing we know for sure, however, is that light *does* affect our health. The

126

human body needs sunshine.

Unfortunately, we do not get the amount of natural light we need, and we may be becoming a grumpy culture because of it. (See CPT No. 37.) Most of us spend 90 percent of our time in buildings and vehicles. In fact, researchers estimate that sixteen hours of artificial lighting provides less emotional benefit than one hour of natural lighting. Lighting—any form of it—can affect your behavior. Here are some enlightening facts:

- In dim light people move at a slower pace and speak more softly than in bright light.
- If lighting is red, people tend to take more risks. When researchers studied the effects of lighting on gambling activity, they found that under red light, gamblers made bigger bets and took greater risks.
- Bright lighting may increase worker productivity, but it may also precipitate boredom, headaches, and eye fatigue.

What's the cheap psychological trick? Take full advantage of natural light when you can. Walk outside during breaks in the clouds, keep curtains open when the sun peeps through, and make sure that the lighting in your workplace is at a healthy level. Remember, even one hour of natural light can brighten your outlook.

REFERENCES

Cunningham, M. R. "Weather, Mood, and Helping Behavior." *Journal of Personality and Social Psychology* 37 (1979) 1947–1956.

Norden, M. J. "Unhappy Holidays?" *Longevity* (1995): 62.

7

Person to Person

Cheap Trick No. 45

Why Not Ask Why?

One word in the English language almost always guarantees a defensive—and less than honest—answer: *why*. That word can strike fear in the hearts of employees, friends, and children alike; and if you say the "w" word with a raised voice, you are bound to run into a brick wall of reticence or a sea of waffling.

Think about the last time you asked a coworker, friend, or child, "Why did you do that?" The response you heard was probably guarded or anxious. Because "why" questions sound accusatory without even trying, as a general rule, "why" questions do not generate straightforward answers and often increase the answerer's anxiety. You end up without the information you need, make others feel self-conscious and defensive, and create an atmosphere of tension and mistrust.

What's the cheap psychological trick? Remove the word "why" from your vocabulary. When you want more information, say, "Tell me more." These three words ask for the same information as a "why" question, but without any of the negative side effects. "Tell me more" is a nonjudgmental solicitation for more information.

You need to be aware, though, of one side-effect of this trick. When you ask people to tell you more, they probably will. That means you may get more information than you really want. But, then, you *did* ask for it!

REFERENCES

Carson, R. C., James N. Butcher, and S. Mineka. *Abnormal Psychology and Modern Life.* New York: HarperCollins, 1996.

Freud, A. *Ego and the Mechanics of Defense* (Revised Edition). International Universities Press, 1967.

Fromm, E. *The Sane Society.* New York: Holt, Rinehart, & Winston, 1955.

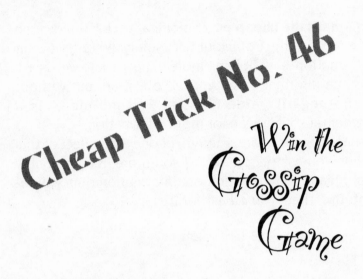

Cheap Trick No. 46

Win the Gossip Game

10 Things You Should Know About Gossip:

- ☆ Everyone gossips. Even if you only listen, you're still gossiping.
- No one ever asks if the information is true. Everyone assumes that it is.
- The greater the potential damage, the faster gossip travels.
- The more you try to tell people that gossip is not true, the more they believe that it is. To paraphrase Shakespeare, if you protest too much, you may only convince people that there must be some truth in the gossip.
- Major decisions have been based on gossip.
- Of all forms of communication, gossip is the most easily distorted.
- Men gossip just as much as women.

132

- People often gossip in order to protect their own reputations. Gossipers may place the focus on someone or something else to direct your attention away from their own actions.
- The more demeaning or hurtful the gossip, the longer it takes for the victim to hear about it.
- Gossip thrives in an atmosphere of secrecy and competition.

Although there may be ten "rules" governing gossip, it only takes one CPT to stop it. This trick is *not* common sense, and it's probably just the opposite of what you think!

Your first instinct upon hearing baseless rumors may be to denounce them unequivocally. Confronting and denying gossip, however, is the least effective technique in stopping it. A refutation makes a gossiper defensive, as he or she may take your comments against the gossip as a personal attack. Unless another person mentions the rumor first, don't bring it up. According to "information-processing theory," denying a rumor also *reminds* others of the rumor, and in that way, the recall or retrieval of the gossip strengthens the belief in it. Repeated hearings make gossip appear more and more like fact.

What's the cheap psychological trick? A simple denial combined with a positive statement about the topic of gossip will often work wonders. This technique forces a shift in the conversation while subtly throwing doubt on the gossip itself. A study of anti-gossip strategies found that focusing on the positive attributes of the person or thing being targeted stopped the gossip in its tracks. If you hear unkind gossip about a close personal friend, lead the speaker to discuss your friend's positive traits. If someone says that they heard Bill took company money, you could respond, "I don't believe it—didn't you hear he was just named 'Employee of the Month'?" If you hear a negative comment about your company or business, swing the conversation around to all the good that has been accomplished by the research and marketing department.

The happy ending? At least when it comes to gossip, you can help good triumph over evil if you know a CPT! If the gossip is true, the facts will come out sooner or later, but if the rumors are false you will have done something to squelch them before innocent people are hurt.

REFERENCES
Rice, B. "Gourmet Worms: Antidote to Rumor." *Psychology Today* August (1981): 20, 83.
Rosnow, R. L., and A. J. Kimmel. "Lives of a Rumor." *Psychology Today* June (1979): 88–92.
Spacks, P. M. "Gossip: How it Works." *Yale Review* 72 (1983): 561.

Cheap Trick No. 47

How and When to Repulse Others

When people encounter something that makes them uncomfortable or is repulsive to them, they usually cringe, cower, or back off as quickly as possible. You can use this instinct to your advantage.

Imagine this situation: Your are at a social gathering. Someone is insistently coming on to you, and the advances are unwelcome. If polite refusals fail to sink in, tell him or her that you're sick, fake a coughing fit, or let spittle drain out of one corner of your mouth. One loud dry heave in the direction of the perpetrator will "hurl" your love attacker across the room in disgust. You should be safe from unwanted advances after that, and you can go home and recuperate. (Don't laugh until you get out of hearing distance!)

Maybe you are out jogging. The endogenous morphines (commonly called "endorphins") are mixing with your blood chemistry and you are feeling a runner's high. All of a sudden your worst fears are realized. An attacker appears from behind the bushes and grabs you. Should you scream? Should you fight? Unless you have been smart enough to take a course in self-defense, you probably won't know what to do. Instead of trying to overpower the attacker, you might instead pretend that you are going to throw up all over him. You don't have to physically throw up, just loudly dry heave like you're out of control. Your attacker may run off in disgust.

Many people also feel uneasy around people who talk to themselves or act emotionally or mentally unstable. This

slurp

is unfortunate; people with these problems can't help their plights. When in danger, however, you can use this prejudice to your advantage. If you're caught in a situation where you think someone may try and harm you, start reciting Shakespeare at the top of your lungs, or sing and dance to your version of the Bunny Hop. You might even act as though you are having a seizure, jerking your body and letting your eyes roll back in your head. Do something that will freak out the perpetrator. Remember, your immediate concern is taking yourself out of a dangerous situation. If doing this involves acting as alarmingly disgusting as possible, pull out all the stops and try all of the gross tricks your brother tried on you when you were a kid.

What's the cheap psychological trick? If you find yourself in a situation where you need to free yourself from people who are bothering or threatening you, disgust them or make them feel uncomfortable. No one wants to be near a person who might vomit on them! That's disgusting!

REFERENCE
Rozin, P., and A. Fallon. "That's Disgusting!" *Psychology Today* July (1985): 60–63.

Cheap Trick No. 48

Flatter Without Sucking Up

Victor Hugo said a humble compliment is "like a kiss through a veil." And wouldn't you know it? This "veiled kiss" has a scientific name. Psychologists call the compliment a "commendatory behavior," and define it as a statement that makes a person believe he or she has received affirmation or a positive evaluation. No matter the name, the simple compliment continues to be one of the most pleasant and desired elements in our conversational lives. We all love to receive compliments. Matched with smiles, they are verbal pats on the back that make us feel appreciated and good about ourselves.

Try complimenting those around you as a form of positive reinforcement. Forget the statistics and give compliments to anyone, anywhere, anytime, but be sure to link the compliment to a specific, concrete event. Why is this link to a specific event important? Vague compliments can sound like insincere flattery. Instead of saying, "Good work," say "Good work on that report this morning." Don't just say, "Nice outfit." Say "That tie looks great with your suit."

What's the cheap psychological trick? For your compliments to be accepted as sincere, they must combine congratulations with a reference to an individual event. When you combine these two elements, your compliments can inspire people to do their best. If, however, you indiscriminately give compliments and expect them to serve as blanket motivators, you are in trouble. Constantly giving compliments that aren't grounded in specifics will backfire; the recipient will not believe the compliment—or you. You'll appear self-serving and insincere; in other words, you will look like a "brown-noser." People will follow you to the ends of the earth if your compliments are real and earned, but only the most gullible will follow a hollow flatterer.

REFERENCES

Curtis, R. C., and K. Miller. "Believing Another Likes or Dislikes You: Behaviors Making the Beliefs Come True." *Journal of Personality and Social Psychology* August (1986): 284–290.

"How'm I Doing?" *Psychology Today* May–June (1996):16.

Knapp, M. L., R. Hopper, and R. Bell. "Compliments: A Descriptive Taxonomy." *Journal of Communication* Fall (1984): 12–31.

Cheap Trick No. 49

Break In Line — And Get Away With It

Breaking in line—what a contemptible thing to want to do! At times, however, you simply must cut in, and on those (hopefully) rare occasions there are tactics to make the experience more pleasant for everyone involved. But before we delve into the trick's application, a little background information is in order.

Imagine you are standing in line for movie or concert tickets. Even though the line wraps around a city block and you are near the end, you optimistically tell yourself that there are enough seats inside for everyone. You are likely to underestimate the number of people between you and the ticket window in order to justify the amount of time spent standing in line and to reassure yourself that you will get a ticket before they sell out. But as you move up the line, your perception starts to change.

As you near the middle of the line, optimism takes a sharp dive and pessimism increases. This is the critical point—a sort of mental point of no return—when you realize that the supply of tickets is finite. Now your brain, beginning to worry, second-guesses itself. You begin to overestimate the number in front of you and doubt the initial judgment made when you were in the back of the line.

Finally, you near the front of the line. The closer you get to the ticket window, the more your "wait worry" begins to disappear. Tickets in hand, you review the time spent in line as a good investment rather than a foolish waste of time. You are now relieved.

After reading this description, can you pick the best place to break in line?

The point where a person breaks in line is called the "point of intrusion." Whether people will allow you to claim a spot ahead of them in line depends on what's going on in their heads. If they are underestimating where they are in line, you have a shot. If they're overestimating the number of people between them and their ticket, you might as well go home. If you can pick the point where the people immediately behind you will be least likely to feel that their chances of getting a ticket are jeopardized, they will very likely let you break.

But where is this "magic" point? One study asked 129 individuals to break in line at railroad ticket counters, betting parlors, and other locations. Less than half of the intruders received *any objections whatsoever* from those already waiting in line. That in and of itself is a rather fascinating finding, especially because this study was done in New York City.

There was one point, however, where line-cutters were regularly rebuffed. Although common sense suggests that this point was near the front of the line, the statistics lead us to a different conclusion. (This is one of those situations where common sense and psychology don't match.) Only 27 percent of people in line objected when someone broke into the front of the line. However, breaking in at the middle and toward the back—where "worry waiting" is beginning to take hold—brought complaints over 73 percent of the time.

What's the cheap psychological trick? The odds are on your side that you will be allowed to break in nearer the front of the line than at the middle or the back. Optimism takes over as people get closer to the front of the line. Feeling secure that they will indeed get a ticket, they don't object when one person breaks in front of them.

Here's another practical application of this CPT, one that is seen every day on highways. You're driving down the interstate and realize that you need to exit about a mile down the road, but that lane is already backed up with cars trying to exit. You decide to get over early and wait your turn. Cars with turn signals flashing continue to zoom by while you wait, and exasperatingly enough, the drivers nearest to the exit let these speed demons break in line. The "zoomers" save five minutes while you sit in traffic. Why do drivers, even those who've waited a while, let the hot-rodders break in line? The psychology at play in the ticket line holds true here as well. The drivers close to the exit are feeling optimistic; they know one more car won't delay them any more than they've already been delayed.

REFERENCES

Bozzi, V. "Mind If I Cut In?" *Psychology Today* April (1987): 21, 24+.

Mann, L., and K. F. Taylor. "Queue Counting: The Effect of Motives upon Estimates of Numbers in Waiting Lines." *Journal of Personality and Social Psychology* 12 (1969) 95–103.

Cheap Trick No. 50

All Kidding Aside

Everybody loves a kidder—at least most of the time. Teasing and joking can be wonderful ways to reduce anxiety, build relationships, and deal effectively with difficult topics. However, what a person chooses to joke about reveals more than you may think.

Kidding or joking tends to soften the seriousness of some problems. Kidding can also protect the joker, disguising his or her real motive. Finally, joking is not random—it is usually predictable. When people are curious or want more information about an important topic or event, joking about the issue allows them to get this information without divulging their true intent. Notice the topics or areas a person kids or jokes about regularly. They are usually the ones that, consciously or unconsciously, are most important to him or her.

What's the cheap psychological trick? Now that you understand the unconscious motivation behind this behavior, you can consciously use "kidding around" to your advantage. Think a friend might be falling in love? Kid him about it and the vehemence of his response may reveal more than you'd expect. Wonder what your new co-worker is really like? Pay attention to the subjects she kids colleagues about and you'll discover what topics *really* interest her.

Remember: if you want information about something, kid someone about it. Confessions often spill out when people want the jokes to stop. By the same token, your jokes can reveal your hidden agendas, so be careful what *you* kid others about as well.

REFERENCES

Goleman, D. "Who Are You Kidding?" *Psychology Today* March (1987): 21, 24+.

Stein, H. "Cutting Words: The Dark Side of Teasing." *Esquire* January (1985): 31, 103.

Ullian, J. A. "Joking at Work." *Journal of Communication* 26 (1976): 129–133.

Cheap Trick No. 51

Find the Truth Behind the Mask

Not so very long ago a major airline needed to fire thousands of employees. Because this company considered itself a "family," the people at the top felt they could not just eliminate their employees—to do so would be tantamount to firing their own children. In the eyes of their employees and their customers they would look like heartless tyrants.

How did the company leaders get around this public relations nightmare? They hired someone to do the dirty work for them, someone to act as "executioner." The top managers felt minimal guilt—even though they had hired the executioner—because they were one step away from the actual firing. The executioner could remove the unwanted "family" members without compunction, because he or she neither knew the employees nor was known by them. The hired gun could do the job without empathizing with the employees' plights.

This technique of detachment is called "deindividuation." Research has shown that individuals or group members who wear masks, hoods, or paint on their faces—who create some shield they can hide behind—are less compassionate and more likely to harm others. Beware of opponents you cannot see, for they can deliver more hurt to you with less hurt to them. You remain an object to them, and they can therefore remain separate from you.

Use these insights to unobjectify yourself and others. Anytime you can unmask a person, he or she is more likely to treat you as a person with desires and fears instead of as an unfeeling object.

When you need to talk with your boss, ask him or her to step from behind the desk and sit with you in front of it. If you let someone hide behind the mask of an official position, he or she will be less compassionate.

People also use the telephone as a mask. If you fear a negative response from someone, using the telephone to discuss the matter almost guarantees a "no." If you deal with an individual face to face, you minimize the chances of a negative answer because then that individual must deal with you as a person rather than as an account number.

If you are intimidated by your physician, ask him or her to take off the white "doctor" coat. This helps prevent physicians from hiding behind the professional mask of the medical establishment. When the doctor stands before you as a fellow human being, chances are he or she will listen to your questions and concerns more sympathetically.

If you are afraid of a medical procedure and you think the person who is to perform the procedure has done it hundreds of times—so often that it has become routine—make sure you introduce yourself and call the person by name several times before the test actually begins. You have established a relationship, and the procedure is no longer routine or rote for the medical personnel.

Using first names rather than titles is another effective way to connect to an individual. "Mr.," "Ms.," "Dr.," and other titles are masks. Give the other person permission to call you by your first name, and then ask if you may use his or her first name as well. If you remove the masks, you reduce the chances of deindividuation. In much the same manner, using nicknames and terms of endearment strips away pretense and brings people closer to each other.

What's the cheap psychological trick? Never let an individual hide behind a mask. Strip away the mask and you return his or her humanity.

REFERENCES

Lightdale, J. R., and D. A. Prentice. "Rethinking Sex Differences in Aggression: Aggressive Behavior in Absence of Social Roles." *Personality and Social Psychology Bulletin* February (1994): 34–44.

Watson, R. I., Jr. "Investigation into Deindividuation Using a Cross-Cultural Survey Technique." *Journal of Personality and Social Psychology* 25 (1973): 342–345.

Zimbardo, P. G. "The Human Choice: Individuation, Reason, and Order Versus Deindividuation, Impulse, and Chaos." *Nebraska Symposium on Motivation.* Edited by W. J. Arnold and D. Levine. Lincoln: University of Nebraska Press, 1969.

Cheap Trick No. 52
Use Embarrassment to Your Advantage

When asked, "What's your most embarrassing moment?" most people can come up with at least a couple of situations that have left them totally abashed. No matter one's station in life, embarrassment can cause self-consciousness, discomfiture, confusion, and a flood of physiological reactions, including a bright red face. Because it is impossible to avoid embarrassment entirely, you must learn how to minimize it, deal with it, and recover from it.

When you are in an embarrassing situation, there are three ways you can deal with it. First, you can walk away, pretending nothing happened and taking no responsibility for the situation. Second, you can try to maintain your aplomb and attempt to fix the situation. Thirdly, you can express your embarrassment and then rectify the situation. One of these three options is the cheap psychological trick; the other two have negative side effects.

Researchers put these three responses to the test when they asked people to observe a series of shopping mishaps. When a shopper knocked over a grocery display and then pretended not to have done it, observers expressed dislike for that individual. The observers also responded unfavorably to those people who maintained their aura of self-confidence and tried to clean up the mess. The observers best liked the individuals who showed their embarrassment. Their embarrassment seemed to act as a nonverbal apology or a kind of appeasement.

What's the cheap psychological trick? Show your embarrassment. In any situation where you can come across as a vulnerable human being, do so. People will like you better when you don't pretend to be superhuman or incapable of error. Embarrassment is not as bad as you think; it's actually rather endearing. So stay alert when you're pushing that loaded grocery cart, but if a display should topple, all is not lost. Use this trick to turn a red face to your advantage.

REFERENCES

Chance, P. "How Embarrassing!" *Psychology Today* December (1988): 18.

Cupach, W. R., S. Metts, and V. Hazleton. "Coping with Embarrassing Predicaments: Remedial Strategies and their Perceived Utility." *Journal of Language and Social Psychology* 5 (1986): 181–200.

Fink, W. L., and B. A. Walker. "Humorous Responses to Embarrassment." *Psychological Reports* 40 (1977): 475–485.

Cheap Trick No. 53

Surprise!

Everybody loves to have a secret "angel," a special person who anonymously does nice things for them. When your work load or worry is reduced because someone stepped in and helped out, or when someone leaves a candy bar on your desk for no apparent reason, it really lifts your spirits.

We all know how much *receiving* these small favors can affect us. But little surprises can have a great many positive side effects for the giver as well as the receiver! Handing out one small surprise can change your mood immediately into a more positive one. This trick can easily work in everyone's favor.

In fact, giving one simple surprise—doing something that's nice and unexpected—can markedly improve a person's mood for about twenty to thirty minutes. Think of the implications.

Research in this area suggests that one effective treatment for normal, everyday moodiness need not involve drugs, therapy, or a large expenditure of funds. It can simply consist of being kind and doing something nice for others.

Here's how it works. If you want to help someone snap out of a bad mood, you could ask, "What's wrong? Do you want to talk about it?" The answer would probably be no. Rather than trying to solve the problem directly, show you care by doing something nice. If you have a bouquet of flowers on your desk, take out a few posies and leave them in your coworker's cubicle. The research suggests that doing something thoughtful for someone is a powerful act and can considerably change the mood of the recipient.

Any spontaneous act of kindness is going to improve the mood of the recipient for at least twenty minutes. The warm glow from a greeting card, note, or positive email lasts about twenty minutes. That may not sound like a long time, but if a person is having a rough day, those moments may make all the difference and guide them toward a more pleasant day.

If you help someone out anonymously, two things happen. The recipient gets a mood elevator for at least twenty minutes. So do you. Preliminary research suggests helping people without telling them gives you a "feel-good" better than a runner's high. Use this CPT on yourself, too. When you find a quarter in a coin return, see a four-leaf clover, receive a compliment from a colleague, hear from a long-lost friend, complete an enormous project on time, or get a good parking place, take time to enjoy these little surprises. Let these random, pleasant experiences raise your spirits for a while.

What's the cheap psychological trick? Do you want to help your friends feel better? You can't constantly control their emotions, but with one surprise—one act of random kindness—you can almost instantaneously turn a frown into a twenty-minute smile. If you do your good deed anonymously, you might find that your own smile lasts even longer.

REFERENCES

Isen, A. M., K. A. Daubman, and G. P. Nowicky. "Positive Affect Facilitates Creative Problem Solving." *Journal of Personality and Social Psychology* June (1979): 1122–1131.

Isen, A. M., M. Johnson, E. Mertz, and G. F. Robinson. "The Influence of Positive Affect on the Unusualness of Word Associations." *Journal of Personality and Social Psychology* June (1985): 1413–1426.

Moss, F. J. "The Hiring Mood." *Psychology Today* November (1988): 26.

Cheap Trick No. 54

Ask the Right Questions

You can use the following well-known "interviewing" tricks to glean more information from someone. These questions are nothing more than CPTs. First you will want to consider your environment. People will only spill their guts in an environment where they feel comfortable. If you try to "interview" them in uncomfortable or inappropriate surroundings, they may feel threatened and clam up.

To get someone to open up, you can try a phrase like, "How do you feel?" This sympathetic approach will often get someone to confide in you. Once the other person is talking, you might follow up with the question, "How can I help?" (Be advised, however, to use this phrase only if you *are* truly willing to help). When you ask how to help, often people will give you more information in case they might decide to take you up on your offer.

155

Another important interviewing trick involves "The Pregnant 'O.'" This approach is designed to elicit more detail or elaboration from someone who is already relating a problem or story. Remember the last time you visited the physician? As you were explaining an amorphous complaint, the medical technician continued to look at you and ask, "Oh?" This questioning "Oh" is merely a way of saying, "Continue." It is an invitation for you to tell more, an indication that someone is evaluating what you've said and desires more information before making a decision or diagnosis. Use this on others as a prod for more facts.

Questions like "What do you think about that?" or "What's your take on the situation?" are helpful because they turn the other person into an expert. Most people will respond well to these questions because such questions make them feel that you value their judgments. They will feel duty-bound to give you a fuller explanation.

Another way to gain new information or call forth an expansion of a story already in progress is simply to say, "I don't understand that." When people hear you say you are confused, they feel compelled to make you understand. They will assume the powerful role of "teacher" to your subservient one as student. (You may learn a lot!)

Think of your reaction when someone responds to you in a teasing way, saying, "I can't believe that!" or "You've got to be kidding!" You probably provide additional information in order to make the person believe you. Try this on others. They might see your question as a gentle challenge for them to convince you. Looking incredulous and asking, "Are you sure?" works in exactly the same way.

If while eliciting information you hear inconsistencies, say nothing. Confronting others with discrepancies in their stories will probably stop conversations in their tracks. Just keep nodding through it, and they will continue to talk.

Simply maintaining silence also works beautifully. People can't tolerate silence. They have a need to keep the conversational volley in motion. If you become silent, others will likely fill the void.

Keep in mind that you have no guarantee that a person is telling the truth. If you notice a lot of blinking, nervous tics, or avoidance of eye contact while someone is talking to you, you may be dealing with a person who does not understand the concept of verisimilitude. (See CPT No. 34.)

If none of these techniques helps, go for the simple, direct approach and use three of the most important words in the human language: "Tell me more."

REFERENCES

Greenspoon, J. "The Reinforcing Effect of Two Spoken Sounds on the Frequency of Two Responses." *American Journal of Psychology* 50 (1955): 409–416.

Leichtman, M.D. "Behavioral Observations." *Clinical Personality Assessment: Practical Considerations.* Edited by J. N. Butcher. New York: Oxford University Press, 1995.

•••••• ❧ ••••••

Love
is a
Four-Letter
Word

♥

♥

♥

♥

Cheap Trick No. 55

Love Is War: Arming Yourself Against "Love Bombers"

There are men and women out there ready to con you and break your heart without a second thought. Given the chance, they will use your kindness and affection against you, taking advantage of your love and your assets. It's hard to believe that you might fall head over heels for someone who has intentions of hurting you, but the truth is that *it happens all the time.*

The people who use your love to get what they want from you are called "love bombers." Before they get you in their clutches, they shower you with love and affection, but once they have you enmeshed in their webs, their black-widow natures emerge.

This trick is not geared toward getting away once you have been caught; the CPT will help you spot these manipulators and avoid getting involved with them. If you think you may be dating a "love bomber," ask yourself the following questions.

- ♡ *Do your friends like him or her?* Almost 100 percent of the time, your friends will hate this guy or gal, but they may not feel comfortable warning you. When you are in the initial throes of love, it's very difficult for friends to tell you anything negative about your new paramour. And if they did try to warn you, the chances are good that you would not listen.

- ♡ *Does the new person you're dating like your friends?* Almost 100 percent of the time, the romantic con will not like your friends. In fact, this type of person will try to turn you *against* your friends; although too subtle to say anything directly, the romantic con will lace his or her conversation with innuendo designed to sour your friendships.

- ♡ *Does this new person in your life encourage you to spend time with your family and friends?* A true romantic con will expend great effort to separate you from your friends, family, children, loved ones—anyone who is important to you. In fact, this question is probably the most important one to ask about your relationship. The con wants to isolate you from anyone who can help you clear your head or act as an objective listener. Remember: the con divides and conquers, all "in the name of love."

- ♡ *Do you know where your partner's money comes from?* A con will likely show you cash, but you'll probably never know where it comes from. If you ask for an explanation, you will most likely hear long tales of sounds-too-good- to-be-true investments. The con is trying to impress you with cash independence. "Love bombers" want to convince you that they have all the resources you need—that you don't need anyone else but them. Once again, the old fence-you-off, divide-and-conquer, reel-you-in, and control-you master plan is at work. But gradually, the money will begin to come from you. As soon as romantic cons realize that their very expensive psychological tricks are working, they will start spending more time away from you. They are already scouting around for the next mark, just in case you wake up and cut them off from your money.

♡ *Is he or she willing to supply you with details you can verify?* Romantic cons avoid describing their pasts or their personal lives; they rarely provide details that you could verify or introduce you to their friends and relatives. They want you to know very little about their past because it is checkered with people (like you) whom they have manipulated. Chances are you're not the first.

♡ *Does your partner have any areas of expertise?* Romantic cons always try to dazzle you with who, what, and how much they know. It may look like they know a great deal, but if you look deeper you will probably discover that they only know a few trivial facts about many subjects. Cons talk a lot but actually say very little.

♡ *Is it hard to predict whether your partner will show you affection, verbally chastise you, or physically attack you?* This sort of confusion, part of the con's master plan, is designed to act on you the way brainwashing works on prisoners of war. The more confused you are about the relationship, the more you may feel your partner needs you. In the beginning your relationship will be marked by "love bombing"—love at every turn. Gradually, verbal abuse will creep in among the declarations of love. Physical assault is often the next step, but you may be tempted to stay because you think there is love between you.

What's the cheap psychological trick? Learn to recognize the warning signs early, talk about your suspicions with people you trust, and then RUN, don't walk, away from romantic cons.

REFERENCES
Carson, R. C., J. N. Butcher, and S. Mineka. *Abnormal Psychology and Modern Life.* New York: HarperCollins, 1996.
Cleckley, H. *The Mask of Sanity* (4th ed.). St. Louis: Mosby, 1964.

Cheap Trick No. 56

Hold Me, Thrill Me, Love Me!

Here's a three-step procedure to use on the one you care for. Hold the object of your desire, add a little thrill, and your companion may love you forever!

The Roman poet Ovid suggested that ladies' hearts were opened when their male suitors took them to gory gladiator contests. You may think his idea is outdated, but it isn't so. Ovid was right.

It is a strange quirk of nature that when human beings encounter a shocking or frightening situation in the company of a possible love interest, they tend to attribute the pounding of their hearts and the butterflies in their stomachs to their feelings for the person they are with. Like Ovid's ladies, they forget that it is probably the violence of the battle that sets their nerves on edge; they believe that inner feelings of love and passion are causing physical disquiet.

But beware—if your date finds you unattractive, the trick can backfire. Instead of interpreting the queasy feelings as passion, your companion may interpret them as disgust! So— before you try this technique, make sure there is a spark of attraction between you and your date.

What's the cheap psychological trick? Take your "love-to-be" on a roller-coaster at an amusement park. The anxiety and thrill of the ride may fan that spark into a flame. If your trip to the amusement park is rained out, suggest a dark, scary movie. It is no mystery why horror films are perennial favorites as date destinations. When your companion grabs your arm, you'll know the magic formula is working!

REFERENCES

White, G. L., S. Fishbein, and J. Rutstein. "Passionate Love and the Misattribution of Arousal." *Journal of Personality and Social Psychology* 41 (1981): 56–62.

Seidman, E. R. "Unusual Romantic Spots." *Redbook* February (1994): 46.

Cheap Trick No. 57

A New Headache Remedy

P leading a headache is one of the most common excuses to avoid sexual relations. But if you really *do* have a headache and refuse sex because of it, you may be missing out on two good things: sexual pleasure and headache relief.

Researchers have found that approximately one in four people with headaches found relief after sex. Why? Perhaps it's as simple as turning one's attention from pain to pleasure. Or perhaps sexual activity and pleasure release the body's natural painkillers, the endorphins. Undoubtedly, scientists will one day discover the answer to this question. But in the meantime, think twice before you say, "Not tonight, dear. I have a headache."

What's the cheap psychological—and physiological—trick? Sexual activity doesn't cure everyone's headaches, but it does at least take your mind off your head and place your attention squarely on alternate parts of your body!

REFERENCE

"Yes, Tonight, Dear; I Have a Headache." *Men's Health* 4 (1988): 10.

Cheap Trick No. 58

Faithful vs. Fatal Attractions

American adults are a randy lot! One study reported the following percentages of individuals in each of four geographic sections of the United States who admitted to at least one extramarital affair:

Midwest	30 percent
Northeast	45 percent
West	48 percent
South	23 percent

Averaged out, these statistics suggest that one out of every three people in the United States has had at least one affair. Dr. Joyce Brothers claimed that two-thirds of married men and half of married women have affairs. To add to the confusion, a Gallup poll reported that nine out of ten married men claimed that they only had sex with their wives. (There was no standard error of measurement or statistical correction for lying in that poll, however.)

No matter which figure is correct, if you're the victim of an affair, you probably feel as if you are the only one in the entire country who has suffered this fate. Here are some signs which will alert you to the probability that your spouse is having an affair. They are not definitive, but Freud was right: it's impossible to keep an affair quiet. Guilty people almost always make a slip, either a physical or a mental one.

Here's what to look for:

- ♡ A *sudden switch in underwear style.* Men having a fling typically go from cotton to silk, or from boxers to bikinis, flaunting their new-found prowess. When women are having affairs, however, they often shift from silky and lacy to cotton and flannel, going out of their way to avoid appearing sexy to their husbands.

- ♡ A *sharp drop in domestic sex drive.* After their daily dalliance, women lose interest in lovemaking at home, and men, subject to penile refractory periods, just don't have the ability after they have strutted their stuff.

- ♡ An *uncharacteristic obsession with laundry chores.* The spouse having an affair may begin to wash his or her own clothes. Washing clothes destroys evidence, like lipstick on the collar or the lingering hint of an unfamiliar perfume or aftershave.

- ♡ New *hobbies that exclude you.* All of a sudden a spouse of fifteen years develops an interest in wines—or takes up fishing, hooks, and lures. The new hobby constantly provides excuses to stay away from home and from you.

- ♡ An *unexpected change in social circles.* Spouses having an **169** affair seem to drop their old friends and begin to hang out with people you've never heard of.

♡ *A sense that your children suspect trouble between mom and dad.* It may be true that the innocent spouse is always the last to know: if you watch your children, you may pick up clues that they know something is wrong long before the truth comes out.

What's the cheap psychological trick? If you are reading (or sending) some of these signals and you feel a lack of communication and a pervasive anxiousness in your household, it is time to take stock of your relationship. Try to discuss your fears with your spouse; if that fails, seek counseling.

It's a pleasure to report that "faithful attractions" still outnumber "fatal attractions." However, like my dear ole grandmother used to say, "Wood don't change its grain." So, when a spouse starts acting different, stay alert. Hopefully you are merely witnessing a mid-life crisis or a renewed interest in life; the most important trick is to keep the lines of communication open.

REFERENCES

Brothers, J. "Why Wives Have Affairs." *Parade* February 1 (1990): 4–7.

Greeley, A. M. *Faithful Attractions.* New York: Tor Books, 1991.

"The Pursuit of Happiness." *Health* March–April (1994): 18.

Cheap Trick No. 59

Improve the ✪Odds of Marital Success

You may know someone who is about to be married. You probably also know someone who will be getting a divorce soon. June may be the month of marriages, but every month is the month of divorces. Is there a way to predict whether your marriage will end in success or failure? Yes, and it's a CPT.

There are five questions to consider that can help predict your marital success.

♡ *Did your parents have a sound marriage?* Statistics show that if they did, it's a plus. If they didn't, that's a strike. People who grew up with a stable family are more likely to form stable families themselves.

♡ *How old are you?* If you marry young, you are more likely to divorce.

♡ *How long have you dated your partner?* The longer you date, the longer you have to determine your potential for compatibility, and the greater the probability that your marriage will succeed.

♡ *How much money do you make*? Mates who struggle with issues of low income are more likely to divorce.

♡ *Are you happy*? If you're not happy before the wedding, you will probably have difficulty working things out after the honeymoon. People who perceive themselves as happy are more likely to be able to cope with adversity.

W **hat's the cheap psychological trick?** Ask yourself these questions before you marry. If you have worked through any emotional negativity and have discussed potential problems before the wedding, you have a better chance for a satisfying married life.

(If all else fails, try this: Take your handkerchief, wash it, and hang it over a rose bush. When it dries in the morning, the initials of your true love and perfect marriage mate will appear in the wrinkles. Sometimes there is just no scientific way to predict what will keep two people together!)

REFERENCES

Amato, P. R. "Long-Term Implication of Parental Divorce for Adult Self-Concept." *Journal of Family Issues* 9 (1988): 201–213.

"Express Yourself." *Psychology Today* March–April (1996): 20.

Glick, P. C., and A. J. Norton. "Marrying, Divorcing, and Living Together in the U. S. Today." *Population Bulletin*, 1977.

Heatherington, E. M. "The Role of Individual Differences and Family Relationships in Children's Coping With Divorce and Remarriage." *Family Transitions.* Edited by P. S. Cowan and E. M. Hetherington. Hillsdale, NJ: Erlbaum Associates, 1990.

"Scotching Marriage." *Psychology Today* March–April (1996): 20.

"Taking the Next Step." *Psychology Today* March–April (1996): 20.

Cheap Trick No. 60

Love Potions

You may not realize it, but you can find aphrodisiacs right in your own kitchen cupboard. Generations of matchmakers have recommended these foods to inspire passion at first bite!

♡ *Apples.* It all started with Adam and Eve, and since the dawn of history poets and storytellers have recounted the powers of this crisp, juicy fruit. In the annals of folklore tradition you will find this advice to lovelorn women: If you want a surefire way to catch a man, take an apple, steep it in your perspiration, and feed it to your chosen one. He will be yours forever. (Of course, it's your decision—you must first be sure that you would be happy with a man who enjoys this sort of thing.)

♡ *Tomatoes.* The French call these fleshy fruits *pommes d'amour,* or love apples. Try serving BLTs at the next candlelight dinner with your mate, and put this time-honored French theory to the test.

♡ *Oranges*. Forget warding off colds. Some say that oranges were the mythological golden apples treasured by the Greeks as food for the gods.

♡ *Chocolate*. This may or may not be a true aphrodisiac, but it tastes so good, who cares? This high-energy food does contain compounds that stimulate the nervous system. The cacao bean had been cultivated in Mexico long before Columbus came to America. According to tradition, the god Quetzylquatl gave it to the Aztecs, and the prophet who ate of the fruit acquired universal wisdom. Apparently believing that such wisdom would enhance his sexual performance, the Aztec emperor Montezuma consumed flagons of the rich sweet drink before entering his harem.

♡ *Vanilla*. When Spanish explore Cortes noticed that the Aztecs enhanced their chocolate with the highly prized vanilla bean, he carried this intoxicating flavor back to Europe. Valued as an aphrodisiac, vanilla soon became the rage. Thomas Jefferson once wrote to a Paris friend asking him to send some of these delectable beans to America.

Do these legendary aphrodisiacs really work? If you mix your love potions with the help of a cheap psychological trick, they can indeed improve your love life.

Offer the aphrodisiac of your choice—anything from a Fudgsicle to an apple—and after lovemaking, praise your partner's performance. At times, most of us feel somewhat vulnerable and insecure during intimate moments. We find it hard to believe that we can provide enough sexual attraction on our own, and we look for aids to help us perform and please our mates. The powerful reinforcement of loving acceptance and praise will enhance the effectiveness of any aphrodisiac. Couple imagination with understanding and you can successfully and repeatedly transform routine lovemaking into a richer experience.

What's the cheap psychological trick? If you love someone, bring a sense of novelty and appreciation to your relationship. This simple combination can work the same wonders as the mythical love potions of the gods.

REFERENCES

Hendrick, C., and J. Hendrick. *Liking, Loving, and Relating.* Monterey, CA: Books/Cole, 1983.

"Love at First Bite." *Ladies' Home Journal* February (1988): 78.

Wilson, J. R., R. F. Kuehn, and F. A. Beach. "Modification in the Sexual Behavior of Male Rats Produced by Changing the Stimulus Female." *Journal of Comparative and Physiological Psychology* 56 (1963): 636–644.

Cheap Trick No. 61

Don't Blame Me!

If you respond negatively to negativity in others, especially those who are closest to you, your friendships and family life are probably fraught with strife. The technical term for the way we respond to others' attitudes is called "attribution." When you are able to attribute an emotion, especially anger, to a situation rather than a person, you can respond positively, or at least rationally, to others. When we blame the situation rather than the person, we are able to remain objective, even in the midst of strife.

Let's say your spouse comes home grumpy and sharp-tongued, pouring out complaints about work, colleagues, you, your home—the world in general. If you can step back and say to yourself "This must have been a really bad day at work" and blame the angry outburst on the situation, you can defuse the negativity and open up a discussion of the issues. If, however, you allow the negative tone to dictate your feelings and responses, if you immediately respond with a negative thought like "Why on earth did I ever marry such a person?" or "I must be doing something really wrong to make him/her so unhappy," if you return mean words with even meaner words, you are closing down the possibility of any fruitful discussion. You may get in the habit of looking for others to blame for bad things, or begin blaming yourself; neither habit does anything to foster understanding between people.

What's the cheap psychological trick? Learn to catch negative thoughts before they take hold and have a chance to grow. Start a conversation; don't close off discussion with negative responses. Don't forget that this trick applies to all relationships, including parenting. Instead of reinforcing your own or others' negative thoughts, bring them out into the open and discuss them. When problems arise, look for the blame in the situation, not in the people involved, and you may be able to turn a potential argument into a positive discussion.

REFERENCES

Bradbury, T. N., and F. D. Fincham. "Attributions in Marriage: Review and Critique." *Psychological Bulletin* 103 (1988): 315–323.

Fletcher, G. J. O., J. Fitness, and N. M. Blampied. "The Link between Attributions and Happiness in Close Relationships: The Roles of Depression and Explanatory Style." *Journal of Social and Clinical Psychology* 9 (1990): 243–255.

"The Wages of Marital Tiffs." *Psychology Today* March–April (1996): 11.

Cheap Trick No. 62

The Love Vaccine

You've probably heard the expression, "An apple a day keeps the doctor away." Now researchers who study the effects of love on the body have put a new spin on the old apple adage. It seems that some affection every day will also keep the doctor away!

Research shows that affectionate actions—in fact, love in general—improve the effectiveness of the immune system. When a person is falling in love, the body produces an amphetaminelike compound called *phenytethylamines* and releases them into the brain. This substance "feeds" your immune system, helping it work more efficiently and effectively. The opposite is also true; researchers have found that the bodies of couples who do not act loving and affectionate with one another have decreased levels of the antibodies and T-cells that keep invading viruses at bay.

What's the cheap psychological trick? Love someone and express that love, and your body will respond by providing healthier chemicals to strengthen your immune system.

If you can't find a person to love, try a pet. It is the *act* of loving and caring that is important, not what the object of your love is. Anytime you have a reason to love, you increase your chances of living longer and enjoying the time you have even more.

Can't find a human, a dog or a cat? Try a plant. Some research suggests that the simple act of tending a garden is good for your body and soul.

So don't let your heart get dusty from lack of use—find someone to love and care for. To adapt another old saying: "An ounce of affection is worth a pound of cure!"

REFERENCE

Ackerman, D. *A Natural History of the Senses*. New York: Random House, 1990.

"The Marriage Benefit—Revisited." *Psychology Today* May–June (1996): 22.

Sheehan, J. "A Kiss a Day Keeps the Doctor Away—Literally." *Longevity* February (1996).

About the Author

Psychologist Perry Buffington's radio show "ParentWise" is heard in many markets. A former contributor to *Delta Airlines Sky* magazine, he has also written for the *Saturday Evening Post*, the *New York Times*, *World Executive Digest*, *New Woman*, and *USA Today*, as well as for corporate employee publications of companies such as UPS, IBM, American Express, and AT&T. He is the author of *Archival Atlanta*; *Your Behavior is Showing*; and *Right Time, Right Place, Right Move, Right Now! 45 Ways to Survive—and Succeed*. Dr. Buffington has also appeared regularly on CNN. He lives in Florida.

About the Illustrator

Mitzi Cartee's work has appeared in *Ms.*, *Utne Reader*, *Special Reports*, and *Storytelling* magazines, as well as in *Home for the Holidays: Stories and Art Created for the Benefit of Habitat for Humanity*. Cartee's rubber stamp designs have been featured in *RubberStampMadness* magazine. A resident of Clemson, South Carolina, she attended Clemson University, the Portfolio Center, and the Greenville Museum School of Art.